EUROPEAN Desserts

LISE NIKORA

ideals®

Ideals Publishing Corp.
Milwaukee, Wisconsin

Contents

Ideals Books

Publisher
Patricia A. Pingry

Managing Editor
Marybeth Owens

Art Director
William Scholz

Production Manager
Mark C. Brunner

Manuscript Editor
Naomi Galbreath

Research Editor
Linda Robinson

Production Assistant
Maureen Treichel

Administrative Assistant
Carmen Johnson

Address all inquiries to:
Ideals Publishing Corporation
11315 Watertown Plank Road
Milwaukee, Wisconsin 53226

Acknowledgments
Editor
Julie Hogan

Photographer
Gerald Koser

Typography
Kim Kaczanowski

Color Separations
MAS Graphics
Menomonee Falls, Wisconsin

Printed By
The Banta Company
Menasha, Wisconsin

Cover Photograph

A classic recipe becomes even more tempting when combined with luscious chocolate frosting . . . Chocolate Torte Black Forest Style (page 17). With its creamy texture and delectable blend of flavors, our showy dessert can become your culinary masterpiece.

Photograph Opposite

Our refreshing Strawberry Cream Torte (page 12) is a delicious addition to any menu. Pretty as a picture, it is sure to earn compliments from family and friends.

Note: Quality can make or break your dessert. There are no substitutes for Kirsch — use Black Forest or Swiss Kirschwasser (cherry spirits); and Framboise — use eau de vie de Framboise or Himbeergeist (raspberry spirits).

Cakes, Tortes, and Flans

Basic Sponge Cake

6 eggs, separated
⅔ cup sugar, divided
1 teaspoon vanilla
1 cup flour, sifted
3 tablespoons unsalted butter, melted and cooled

Butter two 8-inch cake pans with removable bottoms. Line with rounds of parchment paper. Butter and flour parchment paper. Tap out excess flour. Preheat oven to 350° F.

In a small bowl, beat egg whites until soft peaks form. Gradually add about 2 tablespoons of the sugar, beating until stiff peaks form.

In a large bowl, beat egg yolks and remaining sugar until thick and light-colored. Blend in vanilla. Alternately fold in flour and egg whites. Carefully drizzle in melted butter, without pouring in milk solids from bottom of pan. Spread batter evenly in prepared pans.

Bake for 25 to 30 minutes or until golden and a wooden pick inserted in the center comes out clean. Cool in pans on a wire rack for about 15 minutes. Loosen edges of cakes and invert pans onto wire racks. Remove rims and bottoms of pans; peel off paper. Let stand until completely cool. The cakes can be wrapped in plastic wrap and stored at room temperature for several days, refrigerated, or frozen.

Makes 2 layers

Single-Layer Sponge Cake

3 eggs, separated
½ cup sugar, divided
¼ teaspoon vanilla
½ cup flour, sifted
2 tablespoons butter, melted and cooled

Follow directions for Basic Sponge Cake, using these amounts.

Lemon Sponge Cake

Prepare Basic Sponge Cake, substituting the grated peel of 1 lemon for vanilla.

Chocolate Sponge Cake

3 tablespoons unsalted butter
½ cup flour
½ cup unsweetened cocoa
6 eggs, separated
1 cup sugar, divided
1 teaspoon vanilla

Butter two 8-inch cake pans with removable bottoms. Line with rounds of parchment paper. Butter and flour parchment paper. Tap out excess flour. Preheat oven to 350° F.

Melt butter; set aside to cool. Sift together flour and cocoa; set aside. In a small bowl, beat egg whites until soft peaks form. Gradually add about 2 tablespoons of the sugar, beating until stiff peaks form.

In a large bowl, beat egg yolks and remaining sugar until mixture is thick and light-colored. Blend in vanilla. Alternately fold flour mixture and egg whites into egg yolks. Fold in melted butter. Spread batter evenly in prepared pans.

Bake for 25 to 30 minutes or until cake springs back when lightly touched and a wooden pick inserted in the center comes out clean. Cool in pans on a wire rack for about 15 minutes. Loosen edges of cakes and invert pans onto wire racks. Peel off paper. Let stand until completely cool. The cakes can be wrapped in plastic wrap and stored at room temperature for several days, refrigerated, or frozen.

Makes 2 layers

Single-Layer Chocolate Sponge Cake

2 tablespoons butter, melted and cooled
¼ cup flour
¼ cup unsweetened cocoa
3 eggs, separated
⅓ cup sugar, divided
½ teaspoon vanilla

Follow directions for Chocolate Sponge Cake using these ingredients.

Basic Sponge Roll

6 eggs, separated
  Pinch salt
⅔ cup granulated sugar,
  divided
1 teaspoon vanilla
⅔ cup cake flour, sifted
3 tablespoons butter, melted
  Powdered sugar

Butter a 15 x 10-inch jelly roll pan. Line with parchment paper. Butter and flour parchment paper; tap out excess flour. Preheat oven to 350° F.

In a small bowl, beat egg whites and salt until soft peaks form. Gradually add 3 tablespoons of the sugar, beating until stiff peaks form; set aside.

In a large bowl, beat egg yolks and remaining sugar until thick and light-colored. Blend in vanilla. Sift half of the flour over the batter; fold in with a spatula until almost blended. Repeat with remaining flour.

Fold in egg whites and melted butter. Spread batter evenly in prepared pan.

Bake for 15 minutes or until cake is golden and a wooden pick inserted in the center comes out clean. Loosen edges of cake with a sharp knife. Dust a tea towel with powdered sugar. Turn cake out onto towel and peel off paper. Roll up cake with the towel from the wide side. Place on a wire rack to cool completely.

Makes 1 roll

Lemon Sponge Roll

Prepare as above substituting the grated peel of 1 lemon for vanilla.

Chocolate Sponge Roll

6 eggs, separated
  Pinch salt
⅔ cup granulated sugar, divided
½ teaspoon vanilla
⅓ cup sifted cake flour
⅓ cup sifted unsweetened cocoa
¼ cup butter, melted
  Powdered sugar

Follow directions for Basic Sponge Roll, using these amounts. Sift flour and cocoa together before folding into batter.

Lemon-Filled Sponge Roll

1 **Basic Sponge Roll**
  (recipe page 8)
1 **cup unsalted butter**
⅔ **cup granulated sugar**
¼ **cup lemon juice**
  Grated peel of 1 lemon
2 **eggs**
2 **egg yolks**
1 **tablespoon Grand Marnier,**
  optional

Prepare Basic Sponge Roll. Cool in towel on a wire rack; set aside.

In a heavy saucepan (do not use aluminum), combine remaining ingredients, except liqueur. Stir with a wire whisk over low heat until thick and hot. Stir in liqueur. Remove from heat. Place pan in a larger pan filled with ice water; stir until filling is cool. Transfer to a bowl and refrigerate until firm.

On a flat surface, unroll cake. Spread with lemon filling. Reroll by pulling edge of towel up and over. Trim ends. Transfer cake roll, seam side down, to a serving platter. Dust with powdered sugar.

Note: For a slightly stiffer filling, add 1 tablespoon lemon juice to filling ingredients and fold in lightly sweetened whipped cream.

Makes 12 to 14 servings

Refrigerator Cheesecake

1½ **cups graham cracker crumbs**
2 **tablespoons granulated sugar**
¼ **cup unsalted butter, melted**
1 **tablespoon dark rum, optional**
2 **envelopes unflavored gelatin**
½ **cup cold water**
3 **egg yolks**
1⅓ **cups granulated sugar**
½ **cup milk, scalded**
2 **packages (8 ounces each)**
  cream cheese, softened
  Juice of 1 large lemon
  Grated peel of 1 large lemon
2 **cups whipping cream**
2 **tablespoons powdered sugar**

In a small bowl, combine graham cracker crumbs, 2 tablespoons sugar, melted butter, and rum, if desired; blend well. Reserve about ¼ cup for garnish. Press crumb mixture into the bottom and sides of an 8-inch springform pan. Refrigerate crust.

Sprinkle gelatin over water; set aside. In a medium saucepan, beat egg yolks and 1⅓ cups sugar until thick and light-colored. Slowly stir in hot milk. Cook over low heat, stirring constantly, until thickened and custard coats a spoon. Add gelatin; stir until gelatin dissolves. Let stand until lukewarm, stirring frequently.

In a large bowl, beat cream cheese until smooth. Blend in lemon juice and peel; beat until light and fluffy. Gradually blend in custard mixture.

In a large mixing bowl, beat cream until almost stiff. Gradually add powdered sugar and beat until stiff. Fold whipped cream into cheese mixture. Pour into prepared crust. Garnish with reserved crumb mixture. Refrigerate at least 4 hours before serving.

Makes 8 servings

Ribbon Torte

5 eggs, separated
Pinch salt
½ cup granulated sugar, divided
¼ teaspoon vanilla
⅓ cup cake flour, sifted
¼ cup unsweetened cocoa, sifted
3 tablespoons butter, melted

Powdered sugar
Filling
¼ cup currant jelly
3 tablespoons kirsch
1¼ cups whipping cream
¼ cup powdered sugar
1 tablespoon kirsch
2 tablespoons finely grated
chocolate
Chopped or sliced toasted
almonds or Crushed Praline
(recipe page 68)

Follow directions on page 8 for making Chocolate Sponge Roll, using the measurements here for the first 7 ingredients. Bake for 12 to 15 minutes or until a wooden pick inserted in the center comes out clean. Loosen edge of cake with a sharp knife. Turn out onto a sheet of waxed or parchment paper dusted with powdered sugar. Remove pan and paper liner. Cover with a dampened tea towel. Let stand until cool.

Prepare Filling. In a small saucepan, melt jelly. Remove from heat. Blend in 3 tablespoons kirsch.

Remove towel from cake and invert onto a flat surface dusted with powdered sugar; peel off paper.

Brush jelly over cake. Spread filling evenly over top of cake. Refrigerate until filling is firm.

Cut cake lengthwise into strips about 1¾ inches wide. Roll one strip into a coil; stand in the center of a large serving platter. Cut remaining strips in half and carefully wind each strip around the center coil. Cake should be about 10 inches in diameter.

Fasten a paper collar around the cake with tape. Refrigerate until filling is set.

In a mixing bowl, beat cream until partially thickened. Gradually add powdered sugar and beat until stiff. Blend in kirsch. Reserve about ½ cup of the whipped cream mixture; spread remainder over entire cake. Use a fork or pastry comb to draw circular lines over top of cake. Fold grated chocolate into reserved ½ cup whipped cream. Fill a pastry bag fitted with a star tip with whipped cream and pipe rosettes around outer edge and in the center of the cake.

Press toasted almonds or Crushed Praline gently into the sides of the cake. Store in the refrigerator.

Makes 10 servings

Filling

1½ tablespoons unflavored
gelatin
3 tablespoons kirsch
1 tablespoon cold water
2 cups whipping cream
½ cup powdered sugar

In a glass measure, sprinkle gelatin over kirsch and water. Place in a larger pan filled with hot water; stir until gelatin dissolves; set aside.

In a bowl, beat cream until it begins to thicken. Gradually add ½ cup powdered sugar and beat until stiff peaks form. Fold or beat in cooled (but not thickened) gelatin.

Strawberry Cream Torte

1 **Single-Layer Sponge Cake**
   (recipe page 4)
¾ **cup milk**
2 **egg yolks**
¼ **cup sugar**
⅛ **teaspoon vanilla**
1 **tablespoon cornstarch**
2 **tablespoons unsalted butter**
2 **cups whipping cream**
½ **cup powdered sugar or to taste**
1½ **tablespoons kirsch, optional**
   Medium-sized fresh
   strawberries, hulled and rinsed

Prepare Single-Layer Sponge Cake; set aside. In a small saucepan, combine milk, egg yolks, ¼ cup sugar, vanilla, cornstarch, and butter. Cook over low heat, stirring constantly, until mixture coats a spoon. Do not boil. Remove from heat. Place pan in a larger pan of ice water; stir until cool.

In a small bowl, beat whipping cream until it begins to thicken. Gradually add sugar and kirsch, beating until stiff. With a long, serrated knife, slice cake into two layers. Spread pastry cream over bottom layer. Stand strawberries, pointed sides up, over pastry cream. Spoon about half of the whipped cream over the strawberries. Top with second cake layer. Use a large spatula to spread a smooth coating of whipped cream over top and sides of torte. If desired, reserve about ½ cup whipped cream for garnish. Fill a pastry bag fitted with a star tip and pipe rosettes around edge of torte. Place a strawberry in each rosette.

Makes 8 servings

Rich Mocha Torte

2 **Chocolate Sponge Cake layers**
   (recipe page 5)
4 **egg yolks**
1 **cup powdered sugar**
1 **cup unsalted butter, softened**
3 **ounces semisweet chocolate**
½ **ounce unsweetened chocolate**
2 **tablespoons strong coffee**
½ **cup whipping cream**
   Grated unsweetened chocolate
   or chocolate cake crumbs

Prepare Chocolate Sponge Cake; set aside.

In the top of a double boiler, beat egg yolks and powdered sugar until very thick and light-colored. Remove from heat. Gradually beat in butter. In a heavy saucepan over very low heat, melt chocolate in coffee. Blend into buttercream. In a small bowl, beat whipping cream until stiff. Fold into chocolate buttercream.

With a long serrated knife, slice cakes in halves to yield 4 layers. Reserve one layer for another use. Place one layer on a serving plate. Spread with about one-fourth of the buttercream. Top with second layer; spread with buttercream. Repeat with remaining layer and buttercream. Spread remaining buttercream over sides of torte. If desired, reserve a few tablespoons buttercream and fill a pastry bag fitted with a star tip. Pipe small rosettes around the top of the torte and one large rosette in the center. Sprinkle grated chocolate or cake crumbs over the sides of the torte, and gently press into buttercream. Refrigerate until chilled.

Makes 8 servings

Orange Buttercream Torte

2 Basic Sponge Cake layers
   (recipe page 4)
4 egg yolks
1 cup powdered sugar
1 cup unsalted butter, softened
3 tablespoons frozen orange
   juice concentrate, thawed
2 tablespoons Grand Marnier or
   1 tablespoon orange juice
   concentrate
   Orange Glaze
   Orange Syrup
   Toasted almonds, optional
   Chocolate-dipped mandarin
   orange segments, optional

Prepare Basic Sponge Cake; set aside.

In top of double boiler over simmering water, combine egg yolks and powdered sugar. Beat with an electric mixer until thick and light-colored. Remove from heat. Blend in butter, a little at a time. Blend in 3 tablespoons orange juice concentrate and liqueur; set orange buttercream aside.

With a long serrated knife, slice cakes in halves to yield 4 layers. Place bottom layer on a serving plate. Prepare Orange Syrup. Brush part of the syrup over bottom layer. Reserve about one-third of the buttercream. Spread part of buttercream evenly over bottom layer. Top with 2 more layers, spreading each with syrup and buttercream. Press down lightly. Add top layer; brush with remaining syrup.

Prepare Orange Glaze. Pour glaze over top of cake. Use a small spatula to spread evenly. Refrigerate until glaze is set. Spread reserved buttercream over sides of cake, reserving about ½ cup for garnish. Fill a pastry bag fitted with a star tip with reserved buttercream. Pipe rosettes over top of cake, marking 8 slices. Refrigerate until chilled. If desired, press toasted almonds lightly into sides of torte and just before serving, arrange chocolate dipped orange sections on top.

Makes 8 servings

Orange Glaze

¾ cup powdered sugar
1 tablespoon orange juice
   concentrate, thawed
1 to 1½ teaspoons hot water

In a small bowl, combine all ingredients; beat until smooth.

Orange Syrup

2 tablespoons Grand Marnier or
   1 tablespoon frozen orange
   juice concentrate
1 tablespoon water
   (2 tablespoons if using orange
   juice)

Blend together liqueur and water.

Zuger Kirschtorte

1 **Single-Layer Sponge Cake**
  (recipe page 4)
4 **egg whites**
  Pinch salt
3 to 4 **drops lemon juice**
¾ **cup granulated sugar**
½ **cup ground almonds**
  Buttercream
  Kirsch Syrup
  Toasted sliced almonds
  Powdered sugar, optional

Prepare Single-Layer Sponge Cake; set aside. Line two baking sheets with parchment paper. Outline two 8-inch circles on paper. Preheat oven to 275° F. In a small bowl, beat egg whites, salt, and lemon juice until soft peaks form. Gradually add sugar, beating until stiff peaks form. Fold in ground almonds. Spread meringue evenly over the circles. Bake for 40 minutes or until completely dry. Slide paper with meringues onto a flat surface. Let meringue stand until completely cool. Carefully peel off paper. Prepare Buttercream.

Place one of the meringue circles on a serving plate. Spread with about ⅓ of the buttercream. Place sponge cake, bottom side up, over meringue. Prepare Kirsch Syrup. Brush cake with syrup. Spread with another ⅓ of buttercream. Top with second meringue circle; spread remaining buttercream over top and sides of cake. Lightly pat almonds into sides. Dust top of torte with powdered sugar, if desired. Refrigerate until serving time.

Makes 8 servings

Buttercream

4 **egg yolks**
1 **cup powdered sugar**
½ **cup milk, scalded**
1 **cup unsalted butter, room**
  temperature
2 to 3 **tablespoons kirsch**
  (to taste)
2 **tablespoons creme de noyaux**
  or 3 to 4 drops red food
  coloring

In a medium saucepan, beat egg yolks and powdered sugar until thick and light-colored. Slowly stir in hot milk. Return to saucepan. Cook over low heat, stirring constantly, until mixture coats a spoon. Place pan in a larger pan filled with ice water; stir just until lukewarm. Transfer to a large bowl. Beat in butter, a little at a time. Blend in kirsch and creme de noyaux or food coloring.

Kirsch Syrup

1 **tablespoon kirsch**
1 **tablespoon water**

Combine both ingredients in a small cup.

Hazelnut Cream Torte

3 eggs, separated
Pinch salt
½ cup sugar, divided
¼ cup flour, sifted
2 teaspoons unsweetened cocoa
¼ cup ground toasted hazelnuts
1 tablespoon unflavored gelatin
2 tablespoons dark rum or
Frangelico
2½ cups whipping cream
½ cup powdered sugar
⅔ cup Hazelnut Powder
Toasted hazelnuts

Butter an 8-inch cake pan with removable bottom. Line with parchment paper. Butter and flour parchment paper; tap out excess flour. Preheat oven to 350° F.

In a small bowl, beat egg whites and salt until soft peaks form. Gradually add 2 tablespoons of the sugar, beating until stiff peaks form.

In a separate small bowl, beat egg yolks and remaining sugar until thick and light-colored. Sift flour and cocoa together. Alternately fold egg whites and flour mixture into egg yolk mixture. Fold in ground nuts. Spread batter evenly in prepared pan. Bake for 25 to 30 minutes or until a wooden pick inserted in the center comes out clean. Cool in pan on a wire rack for about 15 minutes. Loosen edge of cake and invert onto wire rack. Remove rim and bottom of pan; peel off paper. Let stand until completely cool.

In a 1-cup glass measure, sprinkle gelatin over rum. Place in a larger container filled with hot water; stir to dissolve gelatin. Let stand until cool.

In a large mixing bowl, beat whipping cream and powdered sugar until almost stiff. Pour gelatin mixture into center of the whipped cream; beat until blended and stiff. Fold in Hazelnut Powder.

With a long serrated knife, slice cake into two layers. Place one layer on a serving plate. Spread with a thick layer of whipped cream filling. Press top onto filling. Spread a thin coat of filling over top and sides of torte. Fill a pastry bag fitted with a large star tip with remaining filling. Pipe rosettes or swirls around the top of the torte. Insert a toasted hazelnut into each rosette. Store in refrigerator.

Makes 8 servings

Hazelnut Powder

Follow instructions for Praline (page 68), substituting toasted and skinned* hazelnuts for almonds.

*To skin hazelnuts, preheat oven to 350° F. Place nuts in a single layer on a baking sheet and toast for 12 to 15 minutes. Remove to a tea towel. Gather sides of towel and rub nuts vigorously against each other to remove skins.

Chocolate Torte Black Forest Style

1 **Single-Layer Chocolate Sponge Cake (recipe page 5)**
1 **tablespoon arrowroot**
2 **tablespoons sugar**
1 **can (16 ounces) pitted sour cherries, drained; reserve ½ cup syrup**
4 **tablespoons kirsch, divided**
7 **ounces semisweet chocolate**
2 **cups whipping cream, divided**
⅓ **cup currant jelly, melted**
   Maraschino cherries, optional

Prepare Chocolate Sponge Cake; set aside.

In a small saucepan, combine arrowroot, sugar, and reserved cherry syrup; stir to dissolve arrowroot. Cook over medium heat, stirring constantly, until thick and clear. Add 1 tablespoon kirsch. Pour over cherries in a bowl; stir to coat cherries with glaze.

In a medium saucepan, combine chocolate and ¼ cup of the whipping cream. Melt chocolate over very low heat or over hot water, stirring until smooth. Remove from heat. Let stand until cool. In a small bowl, beat remaining 1¾ cups whipping cream until almost stiff. Stir about 3 tablespoons of the whipped cream into the melted chocolate. Gradually add chocolate to whipped cream; beat until blended and stiff. Do not overbeat.

With a long serrated knife, slice cakes into two layers. Combine melted currant jelly and remaining 3 tablespoons kirsch. Brush half of jelly mixture over bottom cake layer. Arrange sour cherries in an even layer over cake. Spread with about ⅓ of chocolate whipped cream. Top with second cake layer. Spread with remaining jelly mixture. Spread remaining whipped cream over top and sides of torte, swirling for a decorative effect. Garnish with maraschino cherries, if desired. Store in the refrigerator.

Makes 8 servings

Prince Regent Torte

1 recipe Lemon Sponge Cake
  batter (recipe page 4)
  Chocolate Mocha Buttercream
7 ounces semisweet chocolate
1 ounce unsweetened chocolate
1 tablespoon vegetable
  shortening
  Coffee-flavored sweetened
  whipped cream
  Chocolate triangles to
  garnish, optional

Line three large baking sheets with parchment paper. Trace six 9-inch circles on the paper; butter circles and set aside. Preheat oven to 400° F.

Prepare sponge cake batter.

Spoon equal amounts of batter over parchment circles. Bake on center rack for 6 to 8 minutes or until cakes spring back when lightly touched and are golden. Invert cakes onto a floured surface. Peel off parchment paper. Turn cakes upright onto wire racks to cool.

Prepare Chocolate Mocha Buttercream.

Trim cakes with a sharp knife. Spread five of the layers with chocolate buttercream, reserving enough to frost outside of torte; stack on a serving plate. Top with unfrosted layer. Spread remaining buttercream over torte. Refrigerate.

In a small, heavy saucepan, melt chocolates and shortening over low heat. Remove from heat. Let stand until chocolate begins to thicken but is still of pouring consistency. Drizzle glaze over top of torte. Quickly spread glaze over sides of torte. When chocolate is partially set, lightly mark each slice with a sharp knife. Refrigerate until set.

Before serving, fill a pastry bag fitted with a star tip with whipped cream and pipe rosettes over each cake slice. Place a chocolate triangle in each rosette. Refrigerate. Bring cake to room temperature before serving.

Makes 8 servings

Chocolate Mocha Buttercream

4 ounces semisweet chocolate
2 ounces unsweetened chocolate
4 egg yolks
¾ cup powdered sugar
1⅛ cups unsalted butter, softened
1½ tablespoons instant coffee
  powder
3 egg whites
¼ cup superfine sugar

Melt chocolates in a saucepan over hot water; set aside.

In a small saucepan, combine egg yolks and powdered sugar. Place in a larger pan of simmering water; beat with an electric mixer until thick and light-colored. Remove from heat. Beat until lukewarm. Blend in a small amount of butter at a time. Blend in coffee powder and cooled chocolate.

In a small mixing bowl, beat egg whites until soft peaks form. Gradually add sugar and beat until stiff peaks form. Fold egg whites into buttercream.

Apricot Sponge Roll

1 Lemon Sponge Roll
    (recipe page 8)
2¼ cups water
2 cups dried apricots, chopped
1 cup granulated sugar
4 tablespoons apricot liqueur
    or brandy, divided
    Juice of 1 lemon
2 tablespoons milk, heated
1 cup powdered sugar

Prepare Lemon Sponge Roll. Cool in towel on a wire rack; set aside.

In a saucepan, bring water to a boil. Add sugar; stir to dissolve sugar. Add apricots; cook over medium heat, uncovered, until syrup is absorbed, stirring often. Reduce heat, if necessary, to keep from burning. Stir in 3 tablespoons liqueur and lemon juice. Remove from heat. Let stand until cool.

Stir hot milk into powdered sugar until smooth. Add remaining 1 tablespoon liqueur.

On a flat surface, unroll cake. Spread with apricot filling. Reroll by pulling edges of towel up and over. Transfer cake roll, seam side down, to a serving platter. Spread with frosting. Trim ends.
Note: If desired, omit frosting and sprinkle cake with powdered sugar.

Makes 12 to 14 servings

Coconut Lemon Ring

¾ cup unsalted butter
1 cup granulated sugar
4 eggs, separated
    Grated peel of 1 lemon
1½ cups flour
1½ teaspoons baking powder
2 tablespoons milk
½ cup shredded coconut
1 cup powdered sugar, sifted
2 tablespoons lemon juice
3 tablespoons unsalted butter,
    melted

Butter and flour an 8-inch tube pan with a removable bottom; set aside. Preheat oven to 350° F.

In a large mixing bowl, cream butter and sugar until smooth. Add egg yolks, 1 at a time, beating until light and fluffy. Blend in lemon peel. Stir together flour and baking powder. Gradually blend flour mixture into creamed mixture. Blend in milk and coconut.

In a small bowl, beat egg whites until stiff peaks form. Stir about one-fourth of the egg whites into the batter. Fold in remaining egg whites. Turn into prepared pan. Bake for about 1 hour or until a wooden pick inserted near the center comes out clean. Cool cake completely in pan on a wire rack. Loosen edge of cake from pan. Remove rim and pan bottom. Place cake on a serving plate.

In a small bowl, combine powdered sugar, lemon juice, and melted butter; blend until smooth. Let glaze stand 3 to 4 minutes to thicken. Brush glaze over cake.

Makes 16 servings

Orange and Chocolate Cake

4 ounces semisweet chocolate
1 ounce unsweetened chocolate
½ cup unsalted butter, softened
¾ cup granulated sugar, divided
4 eggs, separated
3½ tablespoons orange liqueur, divided
1 cup sifted cake flour
1 egg yolk
⅓ cup powdered sugar
5 tablespoons unsalted butter, softened
Orange and Chocolate Glaze

Butter and flour an 8-inch cake pan with removable bottom; set aside. Melt both chocolates in the top of a double boiler over hot water; set aside. Preheat oven to 350° F.

In a large mixing bowl, cream ½ cup butter and all but 2 tablespoons sugar until light and fluffy. Add 4 egg yolks, 1 at a time, beating well after each addition. Blend in melted chocolate and 2 tablespoons of the liqueur.

In a small mixing bowl, beat egg whites until soft peaks form. Gradually add remaining 2 tablespoons sugar, beating until stiff peaks form. Fold in about ¼ of the egg whites, then alternately fold in flour and remaining whites.

Pour batter into prepared pan. Bake for 30 minutes or until a wooden pick inserted in the center comes out clean. Cool in pan on a wire rack for about 15 minutes. Loosen edge of cake. Remove rim from pan. Do not remove bottom of pan. Cool completely on wire rack.

In a double boiler, beat remaining egg yolk and powdered sugar over simmering water until thick and light-colored. Remove from heat. Beat until lukewarm. Gradually beat in 5 tablespoons butter. Blend in remaining 1½ tablespoons liqueur.

Place cake, still on pan bottom, on a serving plate. Spread buttercream over entire cake. Refrigerate until buttercream is very firm. Or, place cake in freezer until set.

Prepare Orange and Chocolate Glaze. Drizzle glaze over top of cake. Use a metal spatula to spread evenly. Refrigerate until glaze is set.

Makes 8 to 10 servings

Orange and Chocolate Glaze

2 ounces semisweet chocolate
1 tablespoon orange liqueur
¼ cup unsalted butter, softened

Melt chocolate in liqueur over hot water. Gradually blend in butter. Let stand, stirring often, until chocolate begins to thicken but is still of pouring consistency.

Light Lemon Torte

2 **Basic Sponge Cake layers**
  (recipe page 4)
1 **cup unsalted butter, softened**
²₃ **cup sugar**
¼ **cup lemon juice**
  Grated peel of ½ lemon
2 **eggs**
2 **egg yolks**
6 **tablespoons unsalted**
  butter, room temperature;
  divided

Prepare two Basic Sponge Cake layers; set aside.

In a heavy saucepan, combine 1 cup butter, sugar, lemon juice and peel, eggs, and egg yolks. Cook over low heat, stirring with a wire whisk, until thick and hot. Do not boil. Remove from heat. Place pan in a larger pan filled with ice water; stir until cool. Blend in 3 tablespoons of the remaining butter; set lemon cream aside.

With a long serrated knife, slice each cake in half to yield 4 layers; reserve one layer for another use. Place one layer on a serving plate. Spread with ⅓ of the lemon cream. Top with second layer and ⅓ of the lemon cream. Top with third layer. Blend remaining 3 tablespoons butter into remaining ⅓ of the lemon cream. Reserve about ¼ cup lemon cream for garnish. Spread top and sides of cake with lemon cream.

Spoon reserved ¼ cup lemon cream into a pastry bag fitted with a star tip. Pipe small shells around top edge of cake. Pipe a rosette in the center. Top with a thin lemon twist or an unhulled strawberry dipped halfway into melted chocolate. Refrigerate until serving time.

Makes 8 servings

Frankfurter Kranz

5 **egg yolks**
1 **cup powdered sugar**
1⅛ **cups unsalted butter, softened**
1½ **tablespoons dark rum**
¾ **cup Praline Powder**
  (recipe page 43)
½ **cup Crushed Praline**
  (recipe page 68)
1 **chiffon cake (homemade or**
  purchased)
  Sweetened whipped cream
  Maraschino cherries, well
  drained

In top of double boiler over simmering water, combine egg yolks and powdered sugar. Beat with an electric mixer until thick and light-colored. Remove from heat. Beat until lukewarm. Blend in butter, a small amount at a time. Blend in rum and Praline Powder.

With a long serrated knife, slice cake into three layers. Place bottom layer on a serving plate. Spread with about one-fourth of the buttercream. Repeat for remaining layers, reserving enough to frost the outside of the torte. Spread entire cake with remaining buttercream. Refrigerate for 10 to 15 minutes.

Sprinkle some of the Crushed Praline over the top of the cake. Gently press remaining Crushed Praline into sides of cake. Refrigerate until chilled.

Before serving, fill a pastry bag fitted with a star tip with whipped cream and pipe rosettes over the top of the cake. Place a cherry in each rosette.

Makes 16 servings

Raspberry Truffle Torte

1 Single-Layer Chocolate
  Sponge Cake (recipe page 5)
  Chocolate Filling
  (recipe page 38)
5 tablespoons water, divided
2 tablespoons sugar
2 tablespoons framboise, divided
3 ounces semisweet chocolate
2 tablespoons unsalted butter
  Fresh raspberries, optional

Prepare Chocolate Sponge Cake; set aside. Prepare Chocolate Filling; set aside.

In a small saucepan, swirl 2 tablespoons of the water and sugar. Bring to a boil; cook for 2 to 3 minutes. Remove from heat; let stand until cool. Add 1 tablespoon of the framboise.

With a long serrated knife, slice cake into two layers. Brush bottom layer with part of the syrup. Spread filling over bottom layer, reserving about ¾ cup. Press top layer lightly over filling. Brush with remaining syrup. Spread remaining filling over sides of cake. Refrigerate until set.

In a small, heavy saucepan, melt chocolate and remaining 3 tablespoons water over low heat, stirring constantly until smooth. Remove from heat; stir in remaining 1 tablespoon framboise and butter. Let stand until chocolate begins to thicken but is still of pouring consistency. Pour glaze over top of torte. Quickly spread glaze over sides of torte. Refrigerate until chilled.

Garnish with a mound of fresh raspberries placed in the center of the torte before serving.

Makes 8 servings

Imperial Chocolate Cake

1 cup flour, sifted
¼ cup unsweetened cocoa, sifted
2 tablespoons granulated sugar
9 tablespoons unsalted butter,
  chilled
¼ cup cold milk
14 ounces semisweet chocolate
2 ounces unsweetened chocolate
½ cup whipping cream
6 tablespoons unsalted butter,
  softened
2 tablespoons dark rum

In a medium bowl, stir flour, cocoa, and sugar together. Cut in butter with a pastry blender until the mixture resembles coarse crumbs. Add milk, 1 tablespoon at a time, tossing with a fork until dough holds together. Gather dough into a ball. Flatten into a round and wrap in aluminum foil or plastic wrap. Refrigerate for 1 hour. Divide dough into thirds. On a floured surface, roll out each portion into an 8½-inch circle. Place dough rounds on nonstick baking sheets. Chill for 15 minutes. Preheat oven to 400° F.

Prick dough all over with a fork. Bake for 10 minutes or until set. Cool completely on baking sheets.

In a heavy saucepan over low heat, melt chocolates in cream, stirring constantly until smooth. Do not boil.

Remove from heat. Stir in butter and rum. Place pan in a larger pan filled with ice water; stir until of spreading consistency.

Trim cake layers to uniform size. Place one layer on a serving plate. Cover generously with part of the chocolate filling. Add second layer; spread with chocolate filling. Top with third layer. Spread remaining chocolate filling over top and sides of cake. Refrigerate until set. To serve, cut into small wedges with a sharp, thin knife.

Makes 8 servings

Chocolate Hazelnut Log

1 **Chocolate Sponge Roll**
   (recipe page 8)
4 **egg yolks**
½ **cup sugar**
½ **cup milk**
1 **cup unsalted butter, softened**
¼ **cup Hazelnut Paste**
1 **tablespoon strong cold coffee**
1 **tablespoon dark rum**
   Shaved unsweetened chocolate

Prepare Chocolate Sponge Roll. Cool in towel on a wire rack; set aside.

In a medium bowl, beat egg yolks and sugar until thick, light-colored, and doubled in volume. Scald milk in a medium saucepan. Stir hot milk into eggs in a thin stream. Return mixture to saucepan. Stir over low heat until mixture coats a spoon. Do not boil. Remove from heat. Place pan in a larger pan filled with ice water; stir until cool. With an electric mixer, gradually beat in butter. If buttercream separates, add a little more butter. Blend in ¼ cup Hazelnut Paste, coffee, and rum.

On a flat surface, unroll cake. Spread with about two-thirds of the buttercream. Reroll by pulling edge of towel up and over. Transfer cake roll, seam side down, to a serving platter. Spread remaining buttercream evenly over top and sides of cake. Trim ends. Draw a pastry comb or the tines of a fork over the entire length of the cake. Lightly sprinkle with shaved chocolate. Refrigerate until chilled.

Makes 12 to 14 servings

Hazelnut Paste

1 **cup hazelnuts, toasted**
   and skinned

Place hazelnuts in a food processor fitted with a steel knife. Process until nuts are reduced to a paste.

Cafe Mocha Cake Roll

1 **Chocolate Sponge Roll**
   (recipe page 8)
1½ **tablespoons instant coffee**
   powder
¼ **cup boiling water**
1 **tablespoon unflavored gelatin**
1½ **cups whipping cream**
½ **to ⅔ cup powdered sugar**
1 **tablespoon kirsch, optional**
4 **ounces semisweet chocolate**
¼ **cup strong hot coffee**
2 **tablespoons unsalted butter**

Prepare Chocolate Sponge Roll. Cool in towel on a wire rack; set aside.

Dissolve coffee powder in boiling water; let stand until cool. Sprinkle gelatin over cooled coffee. Place gelatin mixture in a larger pan filled with hot water. Stir until gelatin dissolves; set aside.

In a small mixing bowl, beat whipping cream until it begins to thicken. Gradually add powdered sugar, beating until soft peaks form. While beating, pour in gelatin mixture and kirsch; beat until stiff.

Unroll sponge cake on a flat surface. Spread whipped cream evenly over roll to within about ¼ inch of edges. Reroll by pulling edges of towel up and over. Transfer cake roll, seam side down, to a large serving platter. Trim ends.

Combine chocolate and coffee in a small heavy saucepan. Melt chocolate over low heat, stirring constantly. Remove from heat. Stir in butter. If glaze is too thin, let stand until it begins to thicken but can still be poured. Slide narrow strips of waxed paper under the long sides of the cake to catch drippings. Pour glaze slowly over top and sides of cake roll. Use a small spatula to spread glaze evenly. Let stand a few minutes to allow chocolate to partially set. Carefully remove waxed paper. Refrigerate until chilled.

Makes 12 to 14 servings

Kiwi Fruit Flan

1 **Single-Layer Sponge Cake**
   (recipe page 4)
1 **teaspoon superfine sugar**
1 **tablespoon hot water**
2 **tablespoons kirsch, divided**
½ **cup apricot jam, melted and**
   strained
4 **ripe, medium kiwi fruit**
   Raspberries or red currants,
   optional
   Sweetened whipped cream

Prepare Single-Layer Sponge Cake, using a well-buttered and floured 10-inch tart pan. Cool cake in pan for about 15 minutes. Loosen edge of cake. Turn cake out onto a wire rack. Let stand until completely cool; set aside.

Dissolve sugar in hot water. Stir in 1 tablespoon of the kirsch. Place cake on a serving plate. Sprinkle syrup evenly over inside of cake shell. Blend remaining 1 tablespoon kirsch with melted jam. Brush inside of shell with about half of the glaze. Peel and slice kiwi fruit. Arrange kiwi fruit slices in overlapping circles in shell. Brush with remaining apricot glaze. Let stand until set. Garnish with a few small raspberries or red currants, if desired. Serve with whipped cream.

Kiwi Fruit Flan

Makes 6 to 8 servings

Gooseberry Flan

1 **Lemon Sponge Cake layer (recipe page 4)**
1 **tablespoon unflavored gelatin**
¼ **cup water**
2 **tablespoons superfine sugar**
1 **can (16 ounces), gooseberries, drained**
2 **tablespoons Grand Marnier**
1 **tablespoon water**
  Sweetened whipped cream

Prepare Lemon Sponge Cake layer, using a well-buttered and floured 10-inch tart pan. Cool cake in pan for about 15 minutes. Loosen edge of cake. Turn cake out onto a wire rack. Let stand until completely cool; set aside.

In a 2-cup glass measure, sprinkle gelatin over ¼ cup water. Place cup in a larger container filled with hot water; stir to dissolve gelatin. Add sugar; stir until sugar dissolves. Place gooseberries in a medium bowl. Stir in gelatin. Refrigerate until partially set.

Blend together Grand Marnier and 1 tablespoon water. Place shell on a serving plate. Brush inside of shell with liqueur mixture. Spoon gooseberries and gelatin evenly into shell. Refrigerate until set. Fill a pastry bag fitted with a star tip with whipped cream and pipe a lattice top over berries. Serve within 2 hours.

Makes 6 to 8 servings

Apricot Flan

1 **Lemon Sponge Cake Layer (recipe page 4)**
¼ **cup currant jelly, melted**
2 **tablespoons kirsch, divided**
2 **teaspoons unflavored gelatin**
2 **tablespoons water**
1 **can (16 ounces) apricot halves in light syrup, drained; reserve syrup**
  Superfine sugar to taste
  Sweetened whipped cream
  Raspberries or seedless green grapes, optional

Prepare Sponge Cake Layer, using a well-buttered and floured 10-inch tart pan. Cool cake in pan for about 15 minutes. Loosen edge of cake. Turn cake out onto a wire rack. Let stand until completely cool.

Place cake on a serving plate. Blend together jelly and 1 tablespoon of the kirsch. Brush inside of shell with glaze.

In a 2-cup glass measure, sprinkle gelatin over water. Place in a larger container filled with hot water; stir to dissolve gelatin. Stir reserved apricot syrup and remaining 1 tablespoon kirsch into gelatin. Add sugar; stir to dissolve sugar. Refrigerate until partially set.

Arrange apricot halves, hollow sides down, in cake shell. Fill spaces between the apricots with raspberries or grapes. Spoon gelatin mixture evenly over fruit. Refrigerate until set. Fill a pastry bag fitted with a star tip with whipped cream. Pipe rosettes around edge of cake. Serve within 2 hours.

Note: To short-cut this recipe, use a commercially prepared cake shell, adding enough apricot halves to fill.

Makes 6 to 8 servings

Marble Pound Cake

2 cups flour
2 teaspoons baking powder
1 cup unsalted butter, softened
1¼ cups sugar
4 eggs
2 tablespoons dark rum
3 tablespoons unsweetened cocoa, sifted
¼ cup currant jelly
Chocolate Icing

Butter and flour a 9 x 5-inch loaf pan; set aside. Preheat oven to 350° F. Sift flour and baking powder together; set aside.

In a large mixing bowl, cream butter until smooth. Add sugar; beat until light and fluffy. Add eggs, 1 at a time, beating well after each addition. Blend in rum. Gradually fold in flour mixture.

Reserve one-third of the batter. Pour about half of the remaining batter into the prepared pan. Sift cocoa over reserved batter; blend well. Pour chocolate batter over batter in pan. Carefully pour remaining white batter over chocolate batter. Swirl gently with a spatula.

Bake for about 1 hour 15 minutes or until a wooden pick inserted in the center comes out clean. Cool cake completely in pan on a wire rack.

Turn cake out onto a serving plate. Melt jelly in a small saucepan over low heat. Brush melted jelly over entire cake.

Prepare Chocolate Icing. Spread a thin coat of icing over cake. Let stand until set.

Makes 10 to 12 servings

Chocolate Icing

4 ounces semisweet chocolate
2 teaspoons vegetable shortening
2 tablespoons butter, softened

Melt chocolate and shortening in a small saucepan over hot water. Remove from heat. Blend in butter.

Lemon Pound Cake

2 cups flour
2 teaspoons baking powder
1 cup unsalted butter, softened
1¼ cups sugar
4 large eggs, room temperature
Grated peel of 1 large lemon

Butter and flour a 9 x 5-inch loaf pan; set aside. Preheat oven to 350° F. Sift together flour and baking powder; set aside.

In a large mixing bowl, cream butter until smooth. Gradually add sugar, beating until light and fluffy. Add eggs, 1 at a time, beating well after each addition. Blend in lemon peel. Gradually fold in flour mixture. Pour batter into prepared pan. Bake for about 1 hour or until a wooden pick inserted in the center comes out clean. Cool cake completely in pan on a wire rack. Turn out onto a serving plate. Slice and serve.

Makes 10 to 12 servings

Small Sweets and Pastries

Cream Slices

4 eggs, separated
 Pinch salt
½ cup granulated sugar, divided
 Grated peel of ½ lemon
¼ teaspoon vanilla
½ cup cake flour, sifted
 Powdered sugar
2 tablespoons frozen orange
 juice concentrate, thawed
1 tablespoon water
⅓ cup lemon juice
1 tablespoon unflavored gelatin
2½ cups whipping cream
⅔ cup powdered sugar

Butter a 15 x 10-inch jelly roll pan. Line with parchment paper. Butter and flour parchment paper. Preheat oven to 350° F.

In a large mixing bowl, beat egg whites and salt until soft peaks form. Gradually add 2 tablespoons of the sugar, beating until stiff peaks form.

In a separate large bowl, beat egg yolks, remaining 6 tablespoons sugar, lemon peel, and vanilla until thick and light-colored. Alternately fold in flour and egg whites, beginning and ending with flour. Spread batter evenly in prepared pan.

Bake for 12 minutes or until a wooden pick inserted in the center comes out clean. Loosen edges with a sharp knife. Invert cake onto a tea towel dusted with powdered sugar. Remove pan and peel off parchment paper. Let stand until completely cool.

In a small saucepan, dissolve orange juice concentrate in water. Stir in lemon juice. Sprinkle gelatin over orange juice mixture. Place pan in a larger container filled with hot water; stir to dissolve gelatin; set aside.

In a large mixing bowl, beat cream until it begins to thicken. Gradually add ⅔ cup powdered sugar and beat until almost stiff. Pour cooled (but not thickened) gelatin over the whipped cream; beat until stiff.

Cut cake crosswise into two layers. Place bottom layer on a serving plate. Spread filling over bottom layer. Top with second layer. Press together lightly. Smooth sides with a spatula. Dust cake with powdered sugar. Refrigerate until set.

To serve, cut cake into slices or squares. For best results, first cut through the top layer only with the tip of a sharp knife; then cut through the bottom layer.

Makes 16 servings

Almond Horns

1 can (8 ounces) almond paste
1 cup sugar
⅓ cup ground blanched almonds
2 egg whites
1½ cups sliced almonds
    (approximate)
    Granulated sugar
5 ounces semisweet chocolate
1 tablespoon vegetable
    shortening

Break up almond paste in a large bowl. Blend with a fork until smooth. Add sugar, almonds, and egg whites; mix until completely blended and smooth.

Line two baking sheets with parchment paper; set aside. Preheat oven to 300° F.

Break off about 1½ tablespoons of almond batter. Press batter into sliced almonds while shaping into a crescent. Place on baking sheet.

Bake for 20 to 25 minutes or until just lightly browned. Do not overbake. Slide parchment paper onto a flat surface. Let cookies stand for 3 to 4 minutes. Remove horns from paper to a wire rack to cool completely.

In a small saucepan, melt chocolate and shortening over hot water. Dip both ends of horns in melted chocolate. Let stand on a wire rack until chocolate sets.

Makes about 25 servings

Chocolate Porcupines

1 chocolate pound cake,
    homemade or purchased
1 cup whipping cream
2 teaspoons instant coffee
    powder
1 tablespoon Kahlua, optional
18 ounces semisweet chocolate,
    divided
2 tablespoons vegetable
    shortening
    Toasted slivered almonds
    Raisins or semisweet
    chocolate chips
    Unsweetened cocoa

Cut pound cake into slices. Cut each slice into a teardrop shape, the pointed end representing the nose of the porcupine. Cover with plastic wrap and set aside.

In a heavy saucepan, bring cream and coffee powder to a boil. Add 8 ounces chocolate. Stir constantly over low heat until chocolate melts. Remove from heat. Stir occasionally until consistency of pudding. Blend in liqueur. Beat until light and fluffy.

Spoon a large mound of filling over each cake slice, tapering toward the "nose." Refrigerate until firm.

Melt remaining chocolate and shortening in a saucepan over hot water. Place cake slices on a wire rack over a baking sheet. Spoon glaze over cakes; spread with a spatula. Scrape up melted drippings; remelt, and spoon over pastries.

Stud body portion of cakes with almonds to resemble quills. Use raisins or chocolate chips for eyes. Dust noses with cocoa. Let stand until completely set.

Top Hats

5 eggs, separated
⅔ cup granulated sugar, divided
½ cup ground almonds
¾ cup sifted cake flour
2 tablespoons butter, melted
9 ounces semisweet chocolate
2 cups whipping cream, divided
   Powdered sugar
1 tablespoon dark rum or
   1 teaspoon vanilla

Line 24 muffin cups with paper liners; set aside. Preheat oven to 350° F.

In a large bowl, beat egg whites until soft peaks form. Gradually add 2 tablespoons of the sugar and beat until stiff peaks form.

In a separate bowl, beat egg yolks and remaining granulated sugar until thick and light-colored. Blend in almonds. Alternately fold flour and egg whites into egg yolks. Fold in melted butter.

Fill muffin cups about ⅔ full with batter. Bake for 15 to 20 minutes or until cakes are golden and tops spring back when lightly touched. Remove cakes from muffin pans to a wire rack to cool completely. Remove paper liners from cakes. Use a sharp knife to cut tops off cakes in thin slices. Place tops, cut sides up, on a serving plate; cover and set aside.

Make cake shells by carefully scooping out bottom sections of cakes. Discard removed portions and set aside shells.

In a small saucepan, melt chocolate in ½ cup of the cream over hot water, stirring until smooth. Dip shells in chocolate mixture. Place shells, upside down, on a wire rack over aluminum foil; let stand until chocolate is firm.

Before serving, whip cream until it begins to thicken. Gradually add powdered sugar to taste and rum or vanilla and beat until stiff. Spoon or pipe a generous amount of whipped cream onto cake slices. Top with a chocolate frosted shell to complete "hat," allowing some of the whipped cream to show.

Store in the refrigerator.

Makes 24 servings

Filled Meringue Shells

4 egg whites
3 or 4 drops lemon juice
Pinch salt
1 cup superfine sugar
Filling of your choice

Line two large baking sheets with parchment paper. Trace 3-inch circles 1½ inches apart on paper. Fit a pastry bag with a coupler and a ½-inch round opening tip. Preheat oven to 200° F.

In a large bowl, combine egg whites, lemon juice, and salt. Beat with an electric mixer until soft peaks form. Gradually add ½ cup of the sugar and beat until meringue is very stiff and shiny. Sprinkle remaining sugar over egg whites; fold in lightly with a spatula.

Fill prepared pastry bag half-full with meringue mixture. Pipe onto parchment circles, beginning in the center and spiraling outward. Remove plain tip from pastry bag and replace with a ½-inch star tip. Pipe a rim around outside of circles. Bake for 1 hour 45 minutes. Turn off heat and let meringues stand in oven for 1 hour without opening oven door.

Peel paper from shells. Cool shells completely on a wire rack. Store in an airtight container. Can be made 3 days in advance. Serve meringues in any of the following ways.

Note: To form shells without a pastry bag, use a spoon to spread meringue over circles, building up a rim with the back of the spoon.

Makes 10 servings

Kiwi Fruit Lime Meringues

2 egg yolks
¾ cup powdered sugar
2 tablespoons lime juice
¾ cup whipping cream
Sliced kiwi fruit

In the top of a double boiler over simmering water, beat egg yolks, sugar, and lime juice until thick and light-colored. Remove from heat. Beat until cool.

In a small bowl, beat cream until stiff. Fold into custard. Spoon filling into shells and top each with 3 overlapping kiwi fruit slices.

Irish Coffee Meringues

1 cup whipping cream
¼ cup powdered sugar
3 to 4 tablespoons cold triple
  strength coffee
1 tablespoon Irish whiskey

In a small bowl, beat cream until it begins to thicken. Gradually add powdered sugar and beat until stiff. Stir together coffee and whiskey. Blend into whipped cream. Pipe or spoon into meringue shells and serve. Makes filling for 5 to 6 meringue shells.

Coffee Vacherin

⅓ cup whipping cream
2 ounces semisweet chocolate
1 ounce unsweetened chocolate
2 tablespoons coffee liqueur
  or brandy
  Coffee-flavored ice cream

In a small, heavy saucepan, heat cream and chocolates, stirring constantly, until chocolate melts. Blend in liqueur. Spoon slightly softened ice cream into each shell. Top with warm sauce. Serve at once.

Lemon Vacherin

Unhulled whole strawberries
Lemon-flavored ice cream or
custard
Semisweet chocolate, melted

Prepare strawberries by dipping each half-way in melted chocolate. Place on a wire rack over waxed paper until chocolate is firm. Spoon slightly softened ice cream into each shell. Top each with a chocolate-dipped strawberry.

Strawberry Meringues

1 cup whipping cream
3 tablespoons powdered sugar
½ cup strawberry or currant jelly
1 tablespoon kirsch
  Fresh strawberries or partially
  thawed frozen unsweetened
  strawberries

In a small bowl, beat cream until it begins to thicken. Gradually add sugar and beat until stiff.

In a small saucepan, melt jelly over low heat. Stir in kirsch. Pipe or spoon whipped cream into shells. Drizzle jelly over berries.

Rigo Jancsi

10½ ounces semisweet chocolate, divided
⅓ cup flour, sifted
2 tablespoons unsweetened cocoa
4 eggs, separated
⅓ cup sugar
3 or 4 drops lemon juice
Chocolate Filling
⅓ cup apricot jam, melted and strained
¼ cup whipping cream

Lightly butter a 15-inch jelly roll pan. Line with parchment paper. Butter and flour parchment paper; set aside. In a small saucepan, melt 4½ ounces of the chocolate over hot water; set aside to cool slightly. Sift together flour and cocoa; set aside. Preheat oven to 350° F.

In a large bowl, beat egg yolks and sugar until thick and light-colored. Blend in melted chocolate. In a separate bowl, beat egg whites and lemon juice until stiff peaks form. Alternately fold flour mixture and egg whites into egg yolks. Do not overmix. Spread batter in prepared pan. Bake for 15 to 20 minutes or until cake springs back when lightly touched. Let stand for 3 to 4 minutes. Turn out onto a board or tea towel dusted with powdered sugar. Peel off paper. Let stand until completely cool.

Prepare Chocolate Filling.

Cut cake crosswise in half; trim edges. Spread filling over bottom layer. Top with second layer and press down lightly. Smooth sides with a small spatula. Refrigerate until filling is firm.

Spread top with apricot jam. In a small saucepan, melt remaining 6 ounces chocolate in ¼ cup cream over very low heat, stirring until smooth. Pour over top of cake. Quickly spread with a small spatula. Refrigerate until glaze sets.

Cut into 2-inch squares and serve in fluted paper cups, if desired.

Makes about 20 servings

Chocolate Filling

1⅔ cups whipping cream
11 ounces semisweet chocolate
1 ounce unsweetened chocolate
2 tablespoons dark rum or cold strong coffee

In a saucepan, bring whipping cream to a boil. Reduce heat and add chocolates; stir until chocolates melt but *do not boil*. Place pan in a larger container filled with ice cubes, stirring occasionally, until the consistency of pudding. Remove from ice. Add rum; beat until thick and fluffy.

Note: For Raspberry Truffle Torte, use 1¼ cups whipping cream and 7 ounces semisweet chocolate, keeping remaining ingredients the same.

Mocha Petit Fours

7 ounces semisweet chocolate, divided
10 tablespoons hot strong coffee, divided
¾ cup unsalted butter, softened
¾ cup powdered sugar
3 tablespoons unsalted butter
1 frozen chocolate pound cake
1½ tablespoons coffee liqueur
1 tablespoon water

In a small saucepan, melt 1 ounce of the chocolate and 2 tablespoons of the coffee over hot water; set aside. In a large bowl, cream ¾ cup butter and powdered sugar until smooth. Blend in melted chocolate.

Remove pound cake from freezer. Unwrap and let stand for about 5 minutes to thaw slightly. With a long, sharp knife, trim top and sides evenly. Cut cake horizontally into 5 layers. Place one layer on a plate. Combine liqueur and water. Brush some of the liqueur over bottom layer. Spread with a layer of buttercream. Repeat for second layer. Top with a third layer; brush with liqueur mixture. Refrigerate.

Cut remaining two cake layers crosswise in half. Repeat above procedure, using 3 of these layers; refrigerate. Cut the remaining layer into 4 equal parts; discard one part. Brush with liqueur mixture, fill, and stack as above; refrigerate. Reserve a small amount of the buttercream for garnish.

Pour remaining 8 tablespoons coffee over remaining 6 ounces chocolate; stir until chocolate melts. If necessary, briefly place pan over low heat, stirring until chocolate melts. Add 3 tablespoons butter; stir until blended; set aside.

Remove cakes from refrigerator. Use a long sharp knife to cut the largest cake into 10 cubes. Cut the smaller cake into 4 cubes. Set the petit fours about 2 inches apart on a wire rack over a baking sheet or waxed paper. Spoon chocolate glaze over cakes. Quickly spread with a small spatula. Scrape up drippings and remelt; use as needed.

Refrigerate cakes until glaze is partially set. Fill a pastry bag fitted with a star tip with remaining buttercream. Pipe rosettes in the center of each petit four. Return to refrigerator until set. Serve in fluted paper cups, if desired.

Makes 15 servings

Hazelnut Petit Fours

5 eggs, separated
Pinch salt
3 or 4 drops lemon juice
¾ cup granulated sugar, divided
¼ teaspoon vanilla
½ cup sifted cake flour
½ cup ground toasted hazelnuts
Powdered sugar
Whole hazelnuts
Rum Buttercream

Butter a 15 x 10-inch jelly roll pan. Line with parchment paper. Butter and flour parchment paper; set aside. Preheat oven to 350° F.

In a large bowl, beat egg whites, salt, and lemon juice until soft peaks form. Gradually add 3 tablespoons of the sugar and beat until stiff peaks form.

In a separate large bowl, beat egg yolks, remaining sugar, and vanilla until thick and light-colored. Blend in flour. Fold in about ⅓ of the egg whites. Fold in remaining egg whites and ground nuts.

Spread batter evenly in prepared pan. Bake for about 20 minutes or until cake is golden and top springs back when lightly touched. Let stand for 5 minutes. Invert onto a tea towel dusted with powdered sugar. Remove pan and peel off paper. Let stand until completely cool.

Prepare Rum Buttercream.

Cut cake crosswise into two layers. Place bottom layer on a serving plate. Spread with half of the buttercream. Top with second layer. Spread remaining buttercream evenly over top of cake, reserving 3 or 4 tablespoons for garnish.

Draw the tip of a knife through the buttercream to divide the cake into 24 squares. Fill a pastry bag fitted with a star tip with remaining buttercream and pipe a rosette in the center of each petit four. Top each rosette with a whole hazelnut. Refrigerate until set. Cut into squares and serve.

Makes about 24 servings

Rum Buttercream

3 egg yolks
1 cup powdered sugar
⅓ cup milk, scalded
1 cup unsalted butter, softened
2 tablespoons dark rum
½ tablespoon strong coffee

In a small bowl, beat egg yolks and sugar until thick and light-colored. Gradually stir in hot milk; return all to saucepan. Cook over low heat, stirring constantly, until mixture coats a spoon. Remove from heat. Place in a large container filled with ice water. Stir until lukewarm. Beat in butter a little at a time. Blend in rum and coffee.

Pinkies

1 Basic Sponge Roll
  (recipe page 8)
  Powdered sugar
2 egg yolks
½ cup powdered sugar
¾ cup unsalted butter, softened
1½ tablespoons seedless raspberry
  jam
2 to 3 teaspoons framboise or
  kirsch
  Raspberry Frosting

Prepare Basic Sponge Roll. Unmold onto a tea towel dusted with powdered sugar. Peel off paper and let stand until completely cool.

In the top of a double boiler, beat egg yolks and ½ cup powdered sugar until thick and light-colored. Remove from heat. Gradually beat in butter, a little at a time. Blend in jam and framboise.

Use a heart-shaped cookie cutter to cut out small cakes from the entire sponge roll. Use a serrated knife to cut each heart into two layers. Spread ⅓ of the layers with buttercream. Add another layer and buttercream. Top with remaining layers. Refrigerate until filling is firm. Spread remaining buttercream over sides of cakes. Refrigerate until set.

Prepare Raspberry Frosting. Spread frosting over tops of pastries. Refrigerate until set.

Makes about 15 servings

Raspberry Frosting

2 tablespoons milk, heated
1¼ cups powdered sugar
1½ tablespoons seedless raspberry
  jelly, melted

In a small bowl, stir hot milk into powdered sugar; beat until smooth. Blend in melted jelly.

Shoe Soles

1 sheet frozen puff pastry,
  thawed
  Granulated sugar

Roll out pastry on a surface sprinkled with sugar to ⅛-inch thickness. Use a 2-inch round cookie cutter to cut out rounds. Gather scraps together and reroll. Cut out additional cookies. Sprinkle work surface with sugar and turn rounds upside down. Roll each round into an oval. Prick well with a fork. Place pastries on a large baking sheet. Refrigerate for 15 minutes. Preheat oven to 400° F. Bake for 7 to 8 minutes or until golden, watching carefully to avoid burning. Remove from baking sheet to wire racks to cool completely. Store in airtight container. Serve with ice cream or fruit.

Makes about 36 servings

Walnut Roll-Ups

½ cup unsalted butter, softened
4 ounces cream cheese, softened
1 cup flour
1 tablespoon granulated sugar
Pinch salt
Grated peel of ½ lemon
1½ cups ground walnuts
⅓ cup granulated sugar
⅓ cup whipping cream
1½ tablespoons dark rum
½ cup powdered sugar
1 teaspoon lemon juice
2 teaspoons water

In a large bowl, cream butter and cream cheese until smooth. Add flour, 1 tablespoon sugar, salt, and lemon peel; beat until dough holds together. Shape into a 6 or 7-inch block. Wrap in aluminum foil or plastic wrap. Refrigerate overnight or up to several days.

Preheat oven to 375° F. Divide dough into two portions. Roll out each portion on a lightly floured surface into a 13 x 4-inch rectangle. Combine nuts, ⅓ cup sugar, cream, and rum; blend well. Spread nut mixture over dough to within about ½ inch of the edges. Roll up dough from opposite sides toward the center. Lightly pinch center seam together. Place rolls, seam sides down, on a nonstick baking sheet. Bake for about 30 minutes or until golden. Cool on wire rack for 10 minutes. Remove rolls from pan to wire rack to cool completely.

In a small bowl, blend powdered sugar, lemon juice, and water until smooth. Spread over rolls. Cut into 1-inch slices.

Makes about 24

Second-Time-Around Cakes

2½ cups crumbs from leftover chocolate and/or nut cake or crushed macaroon cookies
½ cup currant jelly, or apricot or raspberry jam, melted
3 tablespoons kirsch, rum, or framboise
4 ounces semisweet chocolate
¼ cup hot water
2 tablespoons unsalted butter
2 tablespoons unsalted butter

In a medium bowl, blend crumbs, melted jelly, and kirsch. Divide mixture in half; shape each half into a 2-inch-wide log. Cut into 1½-inch slices. Place slices on a wire rack over aluminum foil.

In a small heavy saucepan, melt chocolate in hot water over low heat. Remove from heat. Blend in butter. Let stand until slightly thickened. Spoon glaze over cakes. Scrape up drippings, remelt and repeat coating until cakes are completely covered with chocolate. If necessary, use a small spatula to spread chocolate on sides. Refrigerate until chocolate is set. Remove to a serving plate with a wide spatula. Store in a cool place.

Makes 6 to 8 servings

Lolitas

½ cup powdered sugar
½ cup granulated sugar
3 egg whites
⅓ cup ground almonds
    Praline Buttercream
5 ounces semisweet chocolate
1 tablespoon vegetable
    shortening

Line two baking sheets with parchment paper; set aside. Fit a pastry bag with a ½-inch round opening tip. Preheat oven to 275° F.

Stir both sugars together. In a small bowl, beat egg whites until soft peaks form. Gradually add sugar and beat until meringue is very stiff and satiny. Fold in almonds. Fill prepared pastry bag with meringue. Pipe 2-inch ovals about 1½ inches apart onto parchment paper.

Bake for 15 to 18 minutes or until shells begin to turn a very pale brown. Remove from oven and slide parchment paper onto a flat surface. Let stand for 10 minutes. Gently peel parchment paper from shells.

Prepare Praline Buttercream.

Over half of the meringue shells, spread a generous amount of buttercream on the flat sides of the shells. Top with remaining shells, flat sides down. Refrigerate until set.

In a small saucepan, melt chocolate and shortening over hot water. Holding the bottom shell of each pastry, dip the top in melted chocolate. Return to refrigerator until chocolate sets. Store in an airtight container in the refrigerator.

Makes about 25 servings

Praline Buttercream

3 egg yolks
⅔ cup powdered sugar
¾ cup unsalted butter, softened
¼ cup Praline Powder
1 tablespoon dark rum

In the top of a double boiler over low heat, beat egg yolks and powdered sugar until thick and light-colored. Remove from heat. Beat in butter, a little at a time. Blend in Praline Powder and rum.

Praline Powder

Prepare Praline (page 68). Break into small pieces. Grind to a fine powder in a blender or food processor. Store any leftover powder in an airtight container in the refrigerator.

Tea Cakes

5 eggs, separated
  Pinch salt
1 cup granulated sugar
  Grated peel of 1 lemon
3 tablespoons orange liqueur
1⅓ cups sifted flour
  Powdered sugar

Line two 9 x 5-inch loaf pans with parchment paper, leaving a 2-inch overhang on ends of pans; set aside. Preheat oven to 350° F.

In a large bowl, beat egg whites until soft peaks form. Add salt and beat until stiff peaks form.

In a smaller bowl, without changing beaters, beat egg yolks until thick and light-colored. Gradually add sugar and beat until smooth. Blend in lemon peel and liqueur. Return flour to sifter. Sift flour over egg mixture, a little at a time, folding in gently with a spatula. Do not over-mix.

Divide batter between prepared pans. Bake for 20 to 25 minutes or until cake springs back when lightly touched. (Cake will be about 2½ inches high.) Cool in pans on a wire rack. Loosen sides with a knife. Remove cake from pan by lifting ends of parchment paper. Invert onto a serving plate and peel off paper. Dust lightly with powdered sugar.

Makes 2 cakes

Sarah Bernhardts

1 can (8 ounces) almond paste
1 cup sugar
2 egg whites
16 ounces semisweet chocolate, divided
1 cup whipping cream
1 tablespoon dark rum
1 tablespoon vegetable shortening

Line two large baking sheets with parchment paper; set aside. Preheat oven to 300° F.

In a large bowl, break up almond paste. Add sugar and egg whites; blend with a fork until smooth. Use 2 teaspoons to drop walnut-size mounds of almond dough onto prepared baking sheet. Or, use a pastry bag fitted with a round opening tip and pipe mounds onto baking sheet. Bake for 20 to 25 minutes or until lightly browned. Slide parchment paper onto a cool surface. Let stand for 3 to 4 minutes to cool slightly. Remove cookies from parchment paper to a wire rack to cool completely. (For best results, bake cookies 2 days before proceeding with recipe.)

In a heavy saucepan over medium heat, melt 8 ounces chocolate in cream, stirring constantly until smooth. Place in a larger container filled with ice cubes; stir occasionally until mixture is the consistency of pudding. Blend in rum. Remove pan from ice. Beat on high speed until thick and fluffy. Spread filling on flat sides of cookies, mounding in the centers. Refrigerate until filling is firm.

In a small saucepan, melt remaining 8 ounces chocolate and shortening over hot water. Dip filling sides of cookies in frosting to cover completely. Refrigerate until chocolate is firm. Store in an airtight container in the refrigerator.

Makes about 45 servings

Benedictine Cakes

4 egg yolks
⅔ cup granulated sugar
2 eggs
1 tablespoon Benedictine
   liqueur
⅔ cup cake flour, sifted
½ cup apricot jam (approximate)
   Benedictine Glaze
   Toasted sliced blanched
   almonds or chopped
   pistachios

Line a muffin pan with paper liners; set aside. Preheat oven to 350° F.

In a large mixing bowl, beat egg yolks and sugar until light and fluffy. Add whole eggs, 1 at a time, beating well after each addition. Blend in liqueur. Fold in flour. Fill muffin cups about one-third full with batter.

Bake for 20 to 25 minutes or until cakes spring back when lightly touched.

While cakes are baking, melt jam in a small saucepan. Strain through a sieve to measure ½ cup.

Brush tops of cakes with apricot jam. Let stand on a wire rack to cool completely.

Carefully remove paper liners from cakes. Spread tops and sides of cakes with Benedictine Glaze. Sprinkle a ring of sliced almonds or chopped pistachios around the top edge of each cake.

Makes 18 servings

Benedictine Glaze

½ cup powdered sugar, sifted
1 teaspoon water
4 teaspoons Benedictine liqueur

In a small bowl, combine all ingredients; blend until smooth.

Cream Puff Paste

1 cup water
6 tablespoons unsalted butter
1 teaspoon sugar
¼ teaspoon salt
1 cup flour
4 eggs

In a heavy saucepan, bring water to a boil. Add butter, sugar, and salt; boil slowly until butter melts. Remove from heat. Add flour all at once. Beat vigorously with a wooden spoon until blended. Return to low heat and beat until mixture forms a ball. Transfer to a warm clean bowl. Let stand 1 to 2 minutes to cool slightly. Add eggs, 1 at a time, beating well after each addition, until smooth and shiny. Use Cream Puff Paste in the following recipes.

Makes about 12 large or 24 small shells, or 22 small eclairs

Orange Puffs with Chocolate Sauce

Cream Puff Paste
(recipe above)
½ cup powdered sugar
  Orange liqueur
4 ounces semisweet chocolate or
  1 ounce unsweetened
  chocolate plus 3 ounces
  semisweet chocolate
1 tablespoon dark rum, strong
  coffee, coffee liqueur, orange
  liqueur, kirsch, or framboise
2 cups whipping cream, divided

Butter and flour two large baking sheets; set aside. Preheat oven to 400° F.

Prepare Cream Puff Paste. Fill a pastry bag fitted with a plain ½-inch round opening tip with Cream Puff Paste. Pipe 1-inch mounds about 2 inches apart onto prepared baking sheets. Bake for 20 minutes or until golden. Turn oven off. Slit each puff to allow steam to escape. Return to oven for 30 minutes to dry out, leaving door partially open.

In a small saucepan, bring 1 cup whipping cream to a boil. Reduce heat. Add chocolate; stir until smooth. Remove from heat. Stir in rum. Set aside.

In a small bowl, beat remaining 1 cup whipping cream until it begins to thicken. Gradually add powdered sugar and beat until stiff. Blend in orange liqueur to taste. Fill a pastry bag fitted with a ¼-inch round opening tip with whipped cream. Fill puffs through a small hole made in the bottom of each puff.

Stack filled cream puffs on a serving plate in a mound. Or, place 3 on each of 5 individual serving dishes. Drizzle sauce over cream puffs and serve.

Makes about 15 servings

Coffee Eclairs

Cream Puff Paste
(recipe page 48)
⅔ cup powdered sugar
2 teaspoons instant coffee
  powder
1 cup whipping cream
1 tablespoon coffee liqueur or
  creme de cocoa
  Coffee Glaze

Butter and flour two large baking sheets; set aside. Preheat oven to 400° F. Prepare Cream Puff Paste. Fill a pastry bag fitted with a ½-inch round opening tip or a star tip with Cream Puff Paste. Pipe 3½ to 4-inch fingers onto prepared baking sheets, cutting batter off with a wet knife. Or, shape batter with two spoons. Bake for 20 minutes or until puffy, golden, and firm. Turn oven off. Remove from oven. Slit the side of each eclair to allow steam to escape. Return to oven for 30 minutes to dry out, leaving door partially open.

Sift powdered sugar and coffee powder together. In a small bowl, beat whipping cream until it begins to thicken. Gradually add powdered sugar mixture and beat until stiff. Blend in liqueur; refrigerate.

Prepare Coffee Glaze.

Slit eclairs horizontally in half. Spread tops with coffee glaze. Place on a wire rack until chocolate is firm.

Spoon filling onto bottoms of eclairs. Cover with chocolate glazed tops and serve.

Makes about 12 servings

Coffee Glaze

⅔ cup powdered sugar
½ teaspoon instant coffee powder
1 teaspoon hot water
1 to 2 tablespoons milk

In a small bowl, combine all ingredients; blend until smooth.

Paris Brest

1 cup Praline Powder
  (recipe page 43)
  Cream Puff Paste
  (recipe page 48)
1¼ cups powdered sugar, divided
½ tablespoon dark rum
½ tablespoon water
  Toasted sliced almonds
2 cups whipping cream

Prepare Praline Powder.

Butter and flour a large baking sheet. Outline an 8-inch circle in the flour; set aside. Preheat oven to 400° F.

Prepare Cream Puff Paste. Fill a pastry bag fitted with a number 7 star tip with Cream Puff Paste. Pipe a ring around the inner edge of the circle. Pipe a second ring just inside the first ring. Pipe a ring directly on top, covering the seam of the two bottom rings. Bake for 40 minutes or until golden. Turn oven off. Make several slits in the pastry to allow steam to escape. Return to

Continued on next page

oven for 30 minutes to dry out, leaving door partially open. Cut pastry horizontally in half. Remove any uncooked dough from center.

In a small bowl, stir together 1 cup of the powdered sugar, rum, and water. Brush rum glaze over outside of top half of pastry. Sprinkle with almonds. Let stand until dry.

In a small bowl, beat whipping cream until it begins to thicken. Gradually add remaining ¼ cup powdered sugar and beat until stiff. Fold in Praline Powder. Fill a pastry bag fitted with a medium star tip with whipped cream. Pipe large rosettes of whipped cream into the bottom of the pastry shell. Or, spoon whipped cream into pastry shell. Replace top.

Makes 6 servings

Cherry Cream Puffs

Cream Puff Paste (recipe page 48)
2 teaspoons arrowroot or cornstarch
¼ cup granulated sugar
1 can (16 ounces) pitted sour cherries, drained; reserve ⅓ cup syrup
1½ cups whipping cream
½ cup powdered sugar
1 tablespoon kirsch, optional

Butter and flour two large baking sheets; set aside. Preheat oven to 400° F.

Prepare Cream Puff Paste. Fill a pastry bag fitted with a large star tip with Cream Puff Paste. Pipe 2-inch mounds about 2 inches apart onto prepared baking sheets. Or, use two spoons to drop dough onto baking sheets. Bake for 30 minutes or until golden. Turn oven off. Slit each puff to allow steam to escape. Return to oven for 30 minutes to dry out, leaving door partially open. Remove cream puffs from oven. Slice off tops and remove any uncooked dough from centers of puffs.

In a small saucepan, combine arrowroot, granulated sugar, and reserved cherry syrup; stir to dissolve arrowroot. Cook over medium heat, stirring constantly, until thick and clear. Pour over cherries in a bowl; stir to coat cherries with glaze.

In a small bowl, beat cream until it begins to thicken. Gradually add powdered sugar and kirsch and beat until stiff.

Spoon a small amount of whipped cream into bottoms of cream puffs. Top with cherries and more whipped cream. Cover with tops of cream puffs and serve.

Makes 6 servings

Apricot Napoleons

1 sheet frozen puff pastry, thawed
1 tablespoon unflavored gelatin
3 tablespoons apricot liqueur
1 cup apricot jam
1½ tablespoons lemon juice
1½ cups whipping cream
3 tablespoons powdered sugar
Apricot Glaze

Roll out puff pastry on a lightly floured surface into an 11 x 14-inch rectangle. Prick well with a fork. Refrigerate for 15 minutes. Preheat oven to 400° F.

Rinse a large baking sheet with cold water. Place pastry on baking sheet. Bake for 10 to 12 minutes or until golden. Slide pastry onto a wire rack. Let stand until cool.

Place pastry on a flat surface. Trim edges with a sharp knife to even sides. Cut crosswise into three pieces.

Sprinkle gelatin over liqueur. Place in a larger container filled with hot water; stir to dissolve gelatin. Let stand until slightly cooled.

In a small bowl, blend jam and lemon juice with an electric mixer. While beating, pour dissolved gelatin into apricot mixture.

In a separate bowl, beat cream until it begins to thicken. Gradually add powdered sugar and beat until stiff. Fold whipped cream into apricot mixture.

Place a pastry piece on a serving plate. Spread with half of the whipped cream mixture. Add another layer of pastry and remaining whipped cream. Top with remaining pastry. Press down lightly and smooth sides with a spatula.

Prepare Apricot Glaze. Spread over top of pastry. Refrigerate until set. Cut into slices and serve.

Makes 6 servings

Apricot Glaze

⅓ cup powdered sugar
2 teaspoons apricot liqueur
½ teaspoon water
3 drops lemon juice

In a small bowl, combine all ingredients; mix until smooth.

Tarts and Tartlets

Tart Shell

1 cup flour
2 tablespoons granulated sugar
   Pinch salt
6 tablespoons unsalted butter,
   chilled and cut in small pieces
½ tablespoon lemon juice
2 tablespoons ice water

In a large bowl, stir together flour, sugar, and salt. Cut in butter with a pastry blender or two knives until consistency of coarse crumbs. Add lemon juice and 1 tablespoon water; toss lightly with a fork. Add remaining 1 tablespoon water and toss until dough holds together. Quickly gather into a ball. Flatten slightly and wrap in plastic or aluminum foil. Refrigerate for at least 2 hours.

On a lightly floured surface, roll out dough into a 9-inch circle. Fold in half and carefully ease into an 8-inch flan ring or cake pan with a removable bottom. Press dough onto bottom and sides of pan. Patch dough, if necessary, by moistening with a little water and pressing edges together. Refrigerate for 30 minutes.

Preheat oven to 375° F. Line unbaked shell with aluminum foil. Fill shell with dried beans or rice. Bake for 20 minutes or until edges begin to brown. Remove beans and foil. Return shell to oven for 8 to 10 minutes or until lightly browned. If shell is to be used with a fruit filling, brush a lightly beaten egg over bottom and sides before returning to oven.

Remove from oven and let stand 3 to 4 minutes to cool slightly. If using flan ring, cool completely in pan on baking sheet. If using a cake pan, carefully remove rim. Transfer shell, still on pan bottom, to wire rack to cool.

Fill baked shell as desired.

Makes 1 shell

Apple Tart

4 to 5 medium tart apples, quartered, peeled, and thinly sliced
5 tablespoons granulated sugar, divided
Grated peel of 1 lemon
2 eggs, separated
⅔ cup sour cream or sour half-and-half
1 baked Tart Shell (recipe page 53)

Preheat oven to 350° F.

In a bowl, sprinkle apples with 2 tablespoons of the sugar and lemon peel, adding additional sugar if apples are very tart.

In a bowl, beat egg whites until stiff peaks form. In a separate bowl, stir together sour cream, egg yolks, and remaining 3 tablespoons sugar; blend well. Fold egg whites into sour cream mixture. Spread apples in baked Tart Shell. Spread topping evenly over apples. Bake for 40 minutes or until golden brown. Cool in pan on a wire rack.

Makes 6 servings

Plum Tart

2 tablespoons currant jelly
1 baked Tart Shell (recipe page 53)
¼ cup granulated sugar
¼ cup water
6 to 8 President plums or purple plums, halved and pitted
1 tablespoon arrowroot
1 tablespoon granulated sugar
1 tablespoon kirsch
Sweetened whipped cream

Brush melted jelly over bottom and sides of Tart Shell; set aside. In a small saucepan, heat sugar and water, stirring until sugar dissolves; set aside.

In a medium saucepan or skillet, place plums in a single layer. Pour sugar water over plums. Bring to a boil. Reduce heat and simmer until tender but firm. Remove plums to a large platter with a slotted spoon. Return accumulated juices to pan.

Combine arrowroot and sugar; stir in ⅔ cup cooled pan juices. Bring to a boil, stirring constantly. Reduce heat. Add kirsch. Cook and stir until sauce is thick and clear. Remove from heat.

Arrange plums, curved sides up, in tart shell. Pour sauce over plums. Refrigerate until chilled. Serve with sweetened whipped cream.

Makes 6 servings

Rhubarb Tart

2 cups cut-up rhubarb
⅓ cup granulated sugar
Pastry Cream
1 baked Tart Shell
(recipe page 53)

Combine rhubarb and sugar in a heavy saucepan. Cook over low heat, stirring occasionally, until rhubarb is tender but firm. Remove from heat. Let stand until cool.

Prepare Pastry Cream and fill Tart Shell. Arrange rhubarb on top of Pastry Cream in a single layer. Serve at once.

Makes 6 servings

Pastry Cream

1 cup milk
3 egg yolks
⅓ cup granulated sugar
¼ teaspoon vanilla
2 tablespoons cornstarch
2 tablespoons unsalted butter,
optional
Orange liqueur

In a saucepan, bring milk to a boil. Cover and set aside.

In a bowl, beat egg yolks, sugar, and vanilla until thick and light-colored. Stir in cornstarch. Stir hot milk into egg mixture in a thin stream. Return to saucepan and bring to a boil, stirring constantly, until thick and mixture coats a spoon. Remove from heat. Stir in butter, if desired. Flavor to taste with orange liqueur.
Note: Pastry Cream can be flavored with almond extract, strong coffee, melted chocolate, grated lemon peel, or fruit-flavored liqueur.

Tropical Fruit Tart

Pastry Cream (recipe above)
Almond Extract
½ cup whipping cream
1 baked Tart Shell
(recipe page 53)
Sliced kiwi fruit
Fresh pineapple slices
¼ cup apricot jam, melted and
strained
1 teaspoon kirsch

Prepare Pastry Cream, substituting almond extract for orange liqueur. Let stand until almost cool. In a bowl, beat whipping cream until stiff. Fold whipped cream into Pastry Cream. Pour into Tart Shell.

Arrange overlapping circles of kiwi fruit slices around outer edge of tart. Arrange pineapple slices next to kiwi. Continue making alternating circles of pineapple and kiwi fruit to center of tart.

Stir together apricot jam and kirsch. Brush glaze over fruit. Serve within 1 hour.

Makes 6 servings

Lemon Cream Tartlets

1 cup whipping cream
1 tablespoon unflavored gelatin
¼ cup water
3 egg yolks
1 cup powdered sugar
¼ cup lemon juice
  Grated peel of ½ lemon
2 tablespoons orange liqueur, optional
12 to 15 baked Tartlet Shells

In a bowl, beat cream until stiff; refrigerate.

Sprinkle gelatin over water. Place in a larger container filled with hot water; stir until gelatin dissolves.

In the top of a double boiler, beat egg yolks and powdered sugar until thick and light-colored. Add gelatin, lemon juice and peel; beat until well blended. Remove from heat. Beat until cool. Blend in liqueur and whipped cream. Spoon filling into Tartlet Shells. Refrigerate until serving time.

Makes 12 to 15 servings

Tartlet Shells

¾ cup flour
¼ cup ground almonds
2 tablespoons granulated sugar
  Pinch salt
  Grated peel of ½ lemon
6 tablespoons unsalted butter, chilled
2½ tablespoons ice water

Follow directions for making dough for Tart Shells (page 53), using ingredients at left. Roll out chilled dough to about ⅛-inch thickness. Cut out pieces about ½ inch larger than 2-inch round or 3-inch oval tart tins. Press dough onto bottom and sides of tart tins and trim edges. Refrigerate for 30 minutes.

Preheat oven to 350° F.

Line each shell with a piece of aluminum foil. Fill with dried beans or rice. Bake for 15 minutes. Remove foil and beans. Bake for about 5 minutes or until golden brown. Slide tins onto a wire rack. Let stand until cool enough to handle. Unmold gently and cool completely. Store shells in an airtight container.

Makes about 15

Macaroon Tartlets

1 can (8 ounces) almond paste
1 cup granulated sugar
2 egg whites
¼ cup ground almonds
2 drops almond extract
15 unbaked Tartlet Shells

In a bowl, break up almond paste with a fork. Add sugar and egg whites; blend until smooth. Blend in almonds and extract.

Preheat oven to 350° F.

Spoon filling into Tartlet Shells, filling about two-thirds full. Bake for 20 minutes or until filling is pale brown. Remove from oven. Let cool to room temperature before removing from tins.

Makes 15 servings

Black Cherry Tartlets

1 tablespoon unflavored gelatin
1 can (16 ounces) pitted black cherries, drained; reserve syrup
3 tablespoons currant jelly, melted
1 to 2 tablespoons kirsch
8 baked Tartlet Shells (recipe page 56)
Sweetened whipped cream

Sprinkle gelatin over ¼ cup of the reserved syrup. Place in a larger container filled with hot water; stir until gelatin dissolves. Stir gelatin into ⅓ cup reserved syrup. Stir in jelly, kirsch, and cherries. Refrigerate until almost set. Spoon mixture into Tartlet Shells. Garnish with rosettes of sweetened whipped cream and serve.

Makes about 8 servings

Hazelnut Tartlets

1 tablespoon unflavored gelatin
⅓ cup cold strong coffee
¾ cup whipping cream
4 egg yolks
⅓ cup powdered sugar
2 tablespoons frangelico, optional
¾ cup Hazelnut Powder (recipe page 16)
12 to 15 baked Tartlet Shells (recipe page 56)

Sprinkle gelatin over coffee. Place in a larger container filled with hot water; stir until gelatin dissolves. In a bowl, beat cream until stiff. Refrigerate.

In the top of a double boiler, beat egg yolks and powdered sugar until thick and light-colored. Add gelatin and beat until well blended. Remove from heat. Beat until cool. Blend in liqueur, Hazelnut Powder, and whipped cream. Spoon filling into Tartlet Shells. Refrigerate until serving time.

Makes 12 to 15 servings

Marzipan Tartlets

½ can (4 ounces) almond paste
¼ cup granulated sugar
2 tablespoons unsalted butter, softened
1 egg
2 tablespoons dark rum
Grated peel of ½ lemon
12 to 15 unbaked Tartlet Shells
2 tablespoons currant jelly, melted

In a bowl, break up almond paste with a fork. Add sugar; blend until smooth. Add butter, egg, rum, and lemon peel; blend well.
Preheat oven to 350° F.

Brush unbaked shells with melted jelly. Spoon filling into Tartlet Shells, filling about half full. Bake for 15 to 20 minutes or until filling is golden brown.

Let cool to room temperature before removing from tins.

Makes 12 to 15 servings

Cookies

Filled Macaroons

1 can (8 ounces) almond paste
3 egg whites
1 cup granulated sugar
2 egg yolks
⅔ cup powdered sugar
10 tablespoons unsalted butter
1 tablespoon dark rum
6 ounces semisweet chocolate
1 tablespoon vegetable
   shortening

Line two large baking sheets with parchment paper; set aside.

In a bowl, break up almond paste with a fork. Add egg whites and sugar; blend until smooth. Or, combine almond paste, egg whites, and sugar in a food processor and process until smooth.

Preheat oven to 350° F.

Use two teaspoons to drop walnut-sized mounds of almond mixture about 2 inches apart onto prepared baking sheet. Bake for 20 to 25 minutes or until macaroons are barely golden. Watch carefully to avoid overbrowning. Slide paper with cookies onto a cool surface. Let stand 3 to 4 minutes to cool slightly. Peel cookies from paper and place on a wire rack to cool completely.

In the top of a double boiler, beat egg yolks and powdered sugar over simmering water until thick and light-colored. Remove from heat. Stir in butter, a little at a time, until smooth. Blend in rum.

Place a generous tablespoon of the filling on the flat sides of half of the macaroons. Top with remaining cookies, pressing lightly to spread filling evenly. Refrigerate until filling is set.

In a small saucepan, melt chocolate and shortening over hot water. Dip macaroons about one-third of the way into the chocolate mixture. Make a quarter turn and dip again. Place on aluminum foil. Refrigerate just until chocolate is set. Store in an airtight container in the refrigerator.

Makes about 12

Madeleines

Melted butter
Flour
3 eggs, separated
Pinch salt
3 drops lemon juice
½ cup granulated sugar, divided
1 teaspoon finely grated fresh lemon peel
⅔ cup flour, sifted
3 tablespoons unsalted butter, melted
Lemon Glaze

Brush inside of madeleine pan with melted butter. Dust with flour and tap out excess. Preheat oven to 350° F.

In a large bowl, beat egg whites, salt, and lemon juice until soft peaks form. Gradually add 2 tablespoons of the sugar and beat until stiff peaks form.

In a separate bowl, beat egg yolks, lemon peel, and remaining 6 tablespoons sugar until thick and light-colored. Alternately fold in flour and egg whites, beginning and ending with flour. Drizzle butter over batter; fold in gently. Place prepared madeleine mold on a baking sheet. Fill about ⅔ full with batter. Bake for 15 minutes or until golden. Unmold by pressing narrow end of cookies. Spread Lemon Glaze over ridged sides of cookies.

Makes about 20

Lemon Glaze

⅔ cup powdered sugar
4 to 5 teaspoons lemon juice

Combine all ingredients; blend until smooth.

Rascals

½ cup granulated sugar
1⅓ cups flour
Grated peel of ½ lemon
½ cup unsalted butter, chilled and cut in small pieces
½ cup grated almonds
1 egg, lightly beaten
Currant or raspberry jelly
¾ cup powdered sugar
1 tablespoon lemon juice
1 to 1½ teaspoons hot water

In a large bowl, combine sugar, flour, and lemon peel; blend well. Cut in butter with a pastry blender or two knives until consistency of coarse crumbs. Stir in nuts. Add egg and cut in until dough clings together. Quickly gather into a ball. Flatten slightly and wrap in plastic or aluminum foil. Refrigerate for at least 1 hour.

Preheat oven to 350° F.

On a lightly floured surface, roll out dough until about ⅛ inch thick. Cut out with a 2-inch round cookie cutter. Place on a nonstick baking sheet. Bake for 10 to 12 minutes or until golden brown. Remove from baking sheet to a wire rack to cool. While still warm, spread half of the cookies with jelly. Top with remaining cookies. In a small bowl, combine powdered sugar, lemon juice and hot water. Beat until smooth. Frost cookies with lemon glaze.

Makes about 2 dozen

Butter "S"

1 cup plus 1 tablespoon
  unsalted butter, softened
⅔ cup granulated sugar
8 egg yolks, divided
  Grated peel of 1 large lemon
3 cups flour

In a large bowl, cream butter and sugar until light and fluffy. Add 6 of the egg yolks, 1 at a time, beating well after each addition. Blend in lemon peel. Gradually add flour; blend well. Gather dough into a ball. Flatten slightly and wrap in plastic or aluminum foil. Refrigerate for about 1 hour.

Preheat oven to 350° F.

Working with about ⅓ of the dough at a time, roll into a 1½-inch log on a lightly floured surface. Cut into ½-inch slices. Roll each slice into a 4-inch rope. Shape ropes into the letter "S." Place on a nonstick baking sheet. Beat remaining 2 egg yolks and brush over cookies. Sprinkle with sugar. Bake for 12 to 15 minutes or until edges are golden brown. Cool slightly on baking sheet. Remove to a wire rack to cool completely.

Makes about 6 dozen

Pretzels

1⅓ cups sifted flour
¼ cup granulated sugar
  Grated peel of ½ lemon
1 egg, lightly beaten
½ cup unsalted butter, chilled
  and cut in small pieces
1 egg, lightly beaten
  Coarse sugar or finely
  chopped almonds
1 egg white, lightly beaten

In a large bowl, combine flour, sugar, and lemon peel. Cut in butter with a pastry blender or two knives until consistency of coarse crumbs. Add the egg; blend well. Quickly gather dough into a ball. On a lightly floured surface, knead dough until smooth. Do not overwork dough. Gather into a ball. Flatten slightly and wrap in plastic or aluminum foil. Refrigerate for at least 2 hours.

Break off tablespoonfuls of dough and roll out on a lightly floured surface into 10-inch ropes. Twist ropes into pretzels. Place on nonstick baking sheets. Refrigerate for 20 minutes.

Preheat oven to 375° F.

Dip tops of cookies in egg white, then in coarse sugar or chopped almonds. Return to baking sheets. Bake for 10 to 12 minutes or until barely golden. Remove from baking sheet to a wire rack to cool.

Makes about 2 dozen

Pretzels
Butter Wreaths, page 64
Three Eyes, page 64

Butter Wreaths

1 cup unsalted butter, softened
⅔ cup granulated sugar
2 egg yolks
Juice of ½ lemon
1¾ cups flour
½ cup ground almonds
Melted semisweet chocolate, optional

In a large bowl, cream butter and sugar until light and fluffy. Add egg yolks, 1 at a time, beating well after each addition. Blend in lemon juice. Stir in flour and almonds. Refrigerate for 30 minutes.

Fill a cookie press fitted with a star tip with chilled dough. Press rings onto a nonstick baking sheet. Refrigerate for about 10 minutes.

Preheat oven to 350° F. Bake for 10 minutes or until golden brown around the edges. Remove from baking sheet to a wire rack to cool. If desired, dip cookies partway into melted chocolate.

Makes 3 dozen

Linzer Tarts

1 cup unsalted butter, softened
½ cup granulated sugar
Grated peel of 1 lemon
2 cups flour
¾ cup ground blanched almonds
1 jar (10 ounces) seedless raspberry jam
1 tablespoon kirsch, optional
Powdered sugar

In a large bowl, cream butter and sugar until light and fluffy. Blend in lemon peel. Stir in flour and nuts; blend well. Gather into a ball. Wrap in plastic or aluminum foil. Refrigerate for at least 4 hours.

Bring dough to room temperature. Preheat oven to 325° F.

Divide into four portions. Working with one portion at a time, roll out on a lightly floured surface until ⅛ inch thick. Cut out with a 2-inch fluted cookie cutter. Repeat for remaining dough. Cut out centers of half of the cookies with a 1-inch cookie cutter. Place cookies on nonstick baking sheets. Bake for 8 to 10 minutes or until barely golden. Remove from baking sheets to a wire rack to cool completely.

Blend jam and kirsch until smooth. Spread a thin coat of jam mixture over whole cookies. Top with cut-out cookies and fill centers with jam mixture. Dust with powdered sugar.

Makes about 30

Three Eyes

Follow directions for Linzer Tarts, cutting out cookie dough with a 3-inch cookie cutter. From half of the cookies, cut out three circles using a thimble. Bake and fill as above.

Greek Butter Cookies

1 cup unsalted butter, softened
⅓ cup powdered sugar
1 egg yolk
2 tablespoons dark rum
2 cups flour
⅓ cup ground blanched almonds
  Powdered sugar

In a large bowl, cream butter and powdered sugar until light and fluffy. Add egg yolk and rum; blend well. Stir in flour and almonds. Refrigerate for 30 minutes.

Preheat oven to 325° F.

Break off walnut-size pieces of dough and shape into rolls. Pull ends down to form crescents. Place on an ungreased baking sheet. Bake for 20 to 25 minutes or until barely golden. Remove from baking sheet and roll in powdered sugar. Place on a wire rack over waxed paper. Dust generously with powdered sugar. Let stand until cool.

Makes about 2 dozen

Filled Cats' Tongues

1 cup unsalted butter, softened
1½ cups powdered sugar
  Grated peel of 1 lemon
1 egg
1 egg yolk
2 cups flour
4 ounces semisweet chocolate
¼ cup whipping cream
2 teaspoons strong coffee

Line two large baking sheets with parchment paper; set aside. Preheat oven to 400° F.

In a large bowl, cream butter and powdered sugar until light and fluffy. Blend in lemon peel. Add egg and egg yolk, 1 at a time, beating well after each addition. Sift flour over batter; stir until blended.

Fill a pastry bag fitted with a ½-inch round opening tip with batter. Pipe 3-inch ropes onto parchment paper on baking sheet about 2 inches apart. Bake for 8 to 10 minutes or until golden brown around edges. Slide paper with cookies onto a cool surface. Let stand to cool slightly. Remove from paper to a wire rack to cool completely.

In a small saucepan, melt chocolate, cream, and coffee over low heat, stirring constantly. Spread the flat sides of half of the cookies with chocolate filling. Top with remaining cookies. Let stand until filling sets. Store in an airtight container.

Makes about 2 dozen

Beehives

2 egg whites
Pinch salt
3 drops lemon juice
1 cup granulated sugar, divided
2 tablespoons unsweetened
   cocoa
   Dash cinnamon or to taste
6 ounces sliced blanched
   almonds, toasted

Line a large baking sheet with parchment paper; set aside. Preheat oven to 300° F.

In a bowl, beat egg whites, salt, and lemon juice until soft peaks form. Gradually add ½ cup of the sugar and beat until stiff peaks form.

In a separate bowl, combine remaining ½ cup sugar, cocoa, and cinnamon; blend well. Sprinkle cocoa mixture over egg whites; fold in gently. Fold in almonds. Use two spoons to drop mounds of batter onto prepared baking sheet. Bake for 25 to 30 minutes or until cookies are firm. Slide paper with cookies onto a cool surface. Let stand to cool slightly. Remove from paper to a wire rack to cool completely.

Makes about 24

Ladyfingers

3 eggs, separated
½ cup granulated sugar, divided
½ teaspoon vanilla or grated
   peel of ½ lemon
⅔ cup sifted cake flour
   Powdered sugar

Butter and flour ladyfinger forms or a large baking sheet; set aside. Preheat oven to 350° F.

In a large bowl, beat egg whites until soft peaks form. Gradually add 2 tablespoons of the sugar and beat until stiff peaks form; set aside.

In a separate bowl, beat egg yolks and remaining 6 tablespoons sugar until thick and light-colored. Blend in vanilla. Gently fold in flour. Fold in egg whites.

Fill a pastry bag fitted with a ½-inch round opening tip with batter. Pipe batter into prepared molds or in 4-inch ropes on baking sheet. Sprinkle generously with powdered sugar. Bake for about 12 minutes or until lightly browned. Cool for 10 minutes in pans before removing to a wire rack to cool completely.

For best results, use within 3 days. Can be stored in an airtight container for up to two weeks.

Makes about 18

Confections

Chocolate Truffles

8 ounces semisweet chocolate
1 ounce unsweetened chocolate
1 cup whipping cream
¼ cup unsalted butter, softened
2 to 3 tablespoons framboise
   Powdered sugar
⅓ cup powdered sugar
⅔ cup unsweetened cocoa

In a heavy saucepan, melt chocolates in cream, stirring occasionally, until mixture is smooth and begins to bubble. Remove from heat. Add butter, a little at a time. Blend in framboise. Place in a larger container filled with ice cubes; stir occasionally until cool. When mixture is thickened, beat with a wire whisk or electric mixer until light-colored and smooth. Refrigerate for 10 minutes or until set.

Use two teaspoons to drop small walnut-size mounds onto prepared baking sheet. Dust hands with powdered sugar and roll mounds into rough balls. If chocolate becomes too soft, refrigerate until firm.

Sift together ⅓ cup powdered sugar and cocoa. Roll truffles in cocoa mixture. After all truffles have been coated, repeat this step. Place truffles in miniature candy cups and refrigerate in an airtight container. Do not remove until just before serving.

Makes about 32

Almond Splinters

4 ounces slivered almonds
8 ounces semisweet chocolate
1 tablespoon vegetable
   shortening

Place almonds on a baking sheet. Toast in oven at 350° F. for 8 to 10 minutes or until golden brown. Remove from oven; let stand until cool.

In a small saucepan, melt chocolate and shortening over hot water, stirring until smooth. Stir in toasted almonds.

Line a baking sheet with aluminum foil. Use two teaspoons to drop small mounds onto prepared baking sheet. Refrigerate until set. Place in miniature paper candy cups and store in a cool place.

Makes about 26

Praline

1 cup slivered almonds
1 cup sugar
¼ cup water (scant)

Place almonds on a baking sheet. Toast in oven at 350° F. for 8 to 10 minutes or until golden brown. Remove from oven; set aside. Butter a large sheet of aluminum foil; set aside.

In a heavy skillet, cook sugar and water until a golden caramel color, stirring frequently and removing crystals from side of pan with a wet pastry brush. Quickly stir in toasted almonds.

Pour onto buttered foil and spread quickly with the back of a wooden spoon. Let stand for at least 2 hours. Break up into pieces and use as is or in recipes using Praline Powder or Crushed Praline.

Crushed Praline

Prepare Praline above. Place between sheets of heavy-duty aluminum foil and crush with a rolling pin.

Florentines

3 tablespoons mixed citrus peel
Flour
9 tablespoons unsalted butter
½ cup sugar
2 tablespoons cream or 1 tablespoon cream plus 1 tablespoon dark rum
1¼ cups blanched sliced almonds
Grated peel of ½ lemon, optional
4 ounces semisweet chocolate
2 teaspoons vegetable shortening

Lightly dust citrus peel with flour; chop finely. Line a 13 x 9 x 2-inch baking pan with aluminum foil. Brush foil with melted butter; set aside. Preheat oven to 425° F.

In a small saucepan, melt 9 tablespoons butter. Add sugar and cream; stir until sugar dissolves. Add almonds and chopped citrus and lemon peels. Bring to a boil; simmer for 2 to 3 minutes. Spread almond mixture in prepared pan using a buttered spatula. Bake for 8 to 10 minutes or until light caramel-colored. Remove pan to a wire rack until mixture is almost firm. Invert onto a sheet of buttered aluminum foil and remove pan. If necessary, let stand until foil can be removed without damaging almond mixture. Working quickly, cut into rounds with a buttered 2-inch cookie cutter, pressing firmly with the palm of your hand. Let rounds cool completely.

In a small saucepan, melt chocolate and shortening over hot water. Use a small spatula to spread chocolate mixture on flat sides of almond rounds. Draw the tines of a fork through the chocolate in a zigzag pattern. Let stand in a cool place until chocolate is firm. Store in an airtight container.

Makes about 15

Marzipan Eggs

1 can (8 ounces) almond paste
1 cup powdered sugar
⅓ cup ground almonds
1 tablespoon light corn syrup
2 tablespoons orange liqueur
6 ounces semisweet chocolate
1 tablespoon vegetable
shortening

In a bowl, break up almond paste; blend with a fork until smooth. Add sugar, almonds, corn syrup, and liqueur; blend well, then knead until smooth. Shape walnut-size pieces of almond mixture into eggs.

In a small saucepan, melt chocolate and shortening over hot water. Dip eggs in chocolate to coat completely. Lift from chocolate with two forks. Place on a wire rack covered with foil or parchment paper. Refrigerate until chocolate is set.

Place eggs in paper candy cups. Store in an airtight container in a cool place.

Makes about 24

Vienna Balls

1 can (8 ounces) almond paste
1 cup powdered sugar
⅓ cup ground blanched almonds
1 tablespoon light corn syrup
2 tablespoons framboise
8 ounces semisweet chocolate,
divided
2 tablespoons whipping cream
1 teaspoon framboise, optional
1½ tablespoons vegetable
shortening

In a bowl, break up almond paste; blend with a fork until smooth. Add powdered sugar, almonds, corn syrup, and 2 tablespoons liquor; blend well, then knead until smooth. Shape walnut-size pieces of almond mixture into balls; set aside.

In a small, heavy saucepan over low heat, melt 2 ounces chocolate in cream, stirring until smooth. Remove from heat. Stir in 1 teaspoon framboise, if desired. Refrigerate until firm.

Turn chocolate mixture out onto a surface dusted with powdered sugar. Roll into a pencil shape. Cut into ⅜-inch-long pieces.

Use the handle of a wooden spoon to press a deep indentation, about ⅔ of the diameter, into each almond ball. Press a piece of chocolate into each indentation. Pinch closed and reroll.

In small saucepan, melt remaining 6 ounces chocolate and shortening over hot water. Dip balls in chocolate. Lift from chocolate with two forks. Place on a wire rack covered with aluminum foil or parchment paper. Refrigerate until set. Trim excess chocolate that accumulates on bottoms of balls.

Place balls in paper candy cups. Store in an airtight container in a cool place.

Makes about 24

Mousses and Molds

Mousse au Chocolat

9 ounces semisweet or
unsweetened chocolate
⅓ cup triple strength coffee
2 tablespoons coffee liqueur
1 cup whipping cream
2 tablespoons powdered sugar
3 egg whites
¼ cup superfine sugar
Shaved semisweet or
unsweetened chocolate

In a saucepan, melt chocolate in coffee and liqueur over hot water, stirring until smooth; set aside.

In a small bowl, beat cream and powdered sugar until soft peaks form. In a separate bowl, beat egg whites until foamy. Gradually add superfine sugar, beating until stiff peaks form. Stir about ⅓ of the whipped cream into the melted chocolate. Pour chocolate over remaining whipped cream; fold in gently until partially blended. Fold in egg whites. Pour mousse into a large serving dish or individual dishes. Refrigerate until set. Before serving, sprinkle with shaved semisweet or unsweetened chocolate.

Makes 6 servings

Chocolate Rum Mousse

1 cup milk
2 egg yolks
⅓ cup granulated sugar
8 ounces semisweet chocolate
2 ounces unsweetened chocolate
3 tablespoons dark rum
1½ cups whipping cream
2 tablespoons powdered sugar

In a small saucepan, bring milk to a boil; cover and set aside.

In a bowl, beat egg yolks and granulated sugar until thick and light-colored. Slowly stir in hot milk. Return all to saucepan and cook over low heat, stirring constantly, until mixture begins to thicken and coats a spoon. Remove from heat. Place in a larger container of ice water and stir until lukewarm.

In a small saucepan, melt chocolate over hot water. Stir into custard along with rum. Stir until cool.

In a small bowl, beat cream and powdered sugar until stiff. Fold about ⅔ of the whipped cream into the chocolate mixture. Reserve remaining whipped cream.

Spoon chocolate mixture into parfait glasses, filling about half full. Spoon in a layer of whipped cream and another layer of chocolate mixture. Refrigerate until chilled.

Makes 6 servings

Apple Charlotte

12 large firm apples (about 5
   pounds), such as Golden
   Delicious or Northern Spies
¼ cup unsalted butter
¼ cup brandy or rum, optional
   Juice of 1 lemon
   Grated peel of 1 lemon
½ cup sugar
⅓ cup apricot jam, strained
10 to 12 slices white sandwich
   bread, crusts removed
   Caramel Sauce or Wine Foam

Peel, quarter, and core apples; cut into thin slices. In a large skillet, melt butter. Add apples and cook over medium heat, stirring occasionally, for 15 to 20 minutes or until apples are tender. Add rum, lemon juice and peel, sugar, and jam. Increase heat to medium-high and cook, stirring constantly, until liquid has evaporated and a knife inserted in apple mixture leaves a mark. (If apples are not cooked long enough, charlotte will collapse when unmolded.) Preheat oven to 400° F. Butter a 1½-quart charlotte mold or straight-sided ovenproof casserole. Butter one side of bread slices. Trim enough bread slices to fit bottom of mold in a decorative pattern, placing buttered sides down in pan. Cut remaining bread in half. Arrange around side of pan, overlapping slightly. Turn apples into prepared mold, packing lightly and mounding in the center. Cover with a round of parchment paper. If bread extends above mold, trim. Bake for about 30 minutes or until bread is golden. Remove parchment paper. Let charlotte cool for at least 20 minutes before turning out onto a serving platter. Serve warm or cold with Caramel Sauce or Wine Foam.

Makes 4 servings

Caramel Sauce

½ cup sugar
2 tablespoons unsalted butter
¾ cup whipping cream
¼ teaspoon lemon juice
1 tablespoon dark rum or
   brandy

In a heavy skillet or saucepan, heat sugar over medium heat until light golden. Remove from heat. Add butter; stir until melted. Return to heat. Stir in cream. Cook until bubbly; cook for about 2 minutes. Stir in lemon juice and rum. Remove from heat.

Wine Foam

1 cup chablis or rhine wine
2 eggs
2 egg yolks
⅓ cup superfine sugar

In a heavy saucepan, combine all ingredients. Beat with a wire whisk over moderate heat until mixture comes to a boil and rises in pan. Remove from heat.
Note: Wine foam can also be served as is in stemmed glasses. Serve immediately after rising.

Salzburger Nockerln

2 egg yolks
1 heaping tablespoon flour
  Grated peel of ½ lemon
½ teaspoon vanilla or 1
  tablespoon dark rum
4 egg whites
  Pinch salt
  Scant ¼ teaspoon lemon juice
3 tablespoons granulated sugar
  Powdered sugar

Butter an ovenproof serving dish or individual serving dishes; set aside. Preheat oven to 350° F.

In a small bowl, beat egg yolks, flour, lemon peel, and vanilla with a spoon until smooth.

In a separate bowl, beat egg whites, salt, and lemon juice until foamy. Gradually add sugar and beat until stiff peaks form. Stir 2 or 3 tablespoons of the egg whites into the yolk mixture. Pour yolks over whites; fold together carefully. Mound mixture in prepared serving dish. Bake for 10 to 12 minutes or until golden on the outside and almost set on the inside. Dust with powdered sugar and serve.

Makes 4 servings

Charlotte Macadamia

1 package ladyfingers (10 to 12)
3 tablespoons water
3 tablespoons granulated sugar
4 tablespoons kirsch, divided
2 ounces semisweet chocolate
2 tablespoons strong coffee
½ cup unsalted butter, softened
1 cup powdered sugar
3 ounces unsalted macadamia
  nuts, ground
1¼ cups whipping cream
  Sweetened whipped cream, or
  favorite chocolate sauce

Separate ladyfingers; set aside. In a small saucepan, bring water and granulated sugar to a boil; cook for 3 minutes, without stirring. Remove from heat. Stir in 2 tablespoons of the kirsch. Brush syrup over flat sides of ladyfingers. Line a 1½-quart charlotte mold or stainless steel mixing bowl with ladyfingers, cutting to fit and placing in mold curved sides out.

In a small saucepan, melt chocolate and coffee over hot water. Blend in remaining 2 tablespoons kirsch.

In a mixing bowl, cream butter and powdered sugar until smooth. Blend in melted chocolate and ground nuts.

In a small bowl, beat cream until soft peaks form. Fold creamed mixture into whipped cream. Spoon into prepared mold, tapping mold against a firm surface several times to settle filling. Cover with a round of parchment or waxed paper. Place a plastic lid or saucer on top to weight it down. Refrigerate overnight.

To unmold, remove paper. Run a thin knife or spatula around the edge of the mold. Invert onto a serving plate. Hold your hands over mold for a few seconds to warm it; lift off mold. Return to refrigerator. Decorate with rosettes of whipped cream or serve with chocolate sauce, if desired.

Frozen Desserts

Double Strawberry Ice Cream

2 cups frozen whole
   strawberries, partially thawed
2 tablespoons kirsch
1 pint strawberry ice cream,
   slightly softened

Reserve 4 berries. Puree remaining berries and kirsch in blender. Gradually add ice cream; blend on medium speed until smooth. Do not liquify. Chop reserved berries and fold into the ice cream. Pour into freezer container. Freeze until firm.

Makes 4 servings

Macadamia Ice Cream

1 cup whipping cream
½ cup powdered sugar
2 tablespoons creme de noyaux
   or dark rum
½ to ¾ cup grated macadamia
   nuts

In a bowl, beat cream until partially thickened. Gradually add sugar, beating until stiff. Blend in liqueur; stir in nuts. Pour into freezer container. Freeze until firm.

Makes 4 servings

Coffee Strawberry Bombe

4 tablespoons kirsch, divided
2 tablespoons water
1 package ladyfingers (10 to 12)
1 pint coffee ice cream, slightly
   softened
1 package (16 ounces) frozen
   strawberries, partially thawed
3 tablespoons superfine sugar
   Sweetened whipped cream

Mix 2 tablespoons of the kirsch with the water. Separate ladyfingers. Lightly moisten the flat sides of ladyfingers with liqueur mixture. Line a 1½-quart stainless steel bowl with ladyfingers, placing curved side out.

Use the back of a large spoon to spread ice cream evenly over ladyfingers. Do not fill center. (If ice cream becomes too soft, return briefly to freezer.) Place mold in freezer.

In a blender or food processor, blend strawberries, remaining 2 tablespoons kirsch, and sugar until smooth. Pour strawberry mixture into center of prepared mold. Cover and freeze 8 hours or overnight.

To unmold, invert bowl onto a serving dish. Wrap a hot, damp towel around the bowl for 3 or 4 seconds. Lift off bowl. Decorate with rosettes of sweetened whipped cream. Serve in wedges.

Makes 8 servings

Double Strawberry Ice Cream;
Macadamia Ice Cream;
Gooseberry Sherbet, page 76;
Lemon Sherbet, page 76

Gooseberry Sherbet

1 can (16 ounces) gooseberries
½ cup superfine sugar
2 to 3 tablespoons kirsch
1 cup whipping cream

Combine gooseberries with their syrup, sugar, and kirsch in blender or food processor; blend until smooth. In a bowl, beat cream until stiff. Fold whipped cream into berries. Pour into freezer container. Freeze until firm.

Makes 4 servings

Lemon Sherbet

¼ cup water
¾ cup granulated sugar
1¾ cups half-and-half
¾ cup lemon juice
2 teaspoons frozen orange juice concentrate, thawed
Lemon twists or fresh mint leaves

In a small saucepan, combine sugar and water. Bring to a boil, swirling syrup, and boil for 3 minutes; let stand until cool. Add half-and-half, lemon juice, and orange juice; whisk until completely blended. Pour into freezer trays. Freeze until firm around edges. Transfer to a bowl; beat until smooth. Pour into a freezer container. Freeze until firm. Serve in individual dishes, garnished with lemon twists or fresh mint leaves.

Makes 6 servings

Peach Sorbet

½ cup granulated sugar
½ cup water
1 package (16 ounces) frozen peaches, partially thawed
¼ cup apricot jam
3 tablespoons apricot liqueur, optional

In a small saucepan, combine sugar and water. Bring to a boil, swirling syrup, and boil 3 minutes. Remove from heat. Let stand until cool. In a blender or food processor, combine peaches, syrup, jam, and liqueur; blend until smooth. Pour into a freezer container. Freeze until firm around edges. Whip with a fork until smooth. Return to freezer until firm.

Makes 4 servings

Raspberry Sorbet

1 package (16 ounces) frozen raspberries in syrup, partially thawed
⅓ cup currant jelly
2 tablespoons framboise, kirsch or creme de cassis

In a blender or food processor, combine all ingredients; blend until smooth. Strain berry mixture. Pour into freezer container. Freeze until firm around edges. Whip with a fork until smooth. Return to freezer until firm.

Makes 4 servings

Fruit Desserts

Flamed Bananas

3 tablespoons unsalted butter
2 tablespoons granulated sugar
1 tablespoon frozen orange juice concentrate, thawed
1 teaspoon lemon juice
4 large ripe bananas, cut in half vertically
1 tablespoon dark rum
Hot chocolate sauce

In a chafing dish or large skillet, melt butter. Add sugar; stir until dissolved. Add orange and lemon juice. Poach bananas in sauce, turning occasionally, until heated but still firm. Add rum and ignite. Spoon flaming liquid over bananas until flames die. Serve with hot chocolate sauce.

Makes 4 servings

Fruit Salad

This dessert can be made entirely of fresh fruit, or of a combination of fresh and canned fruit. Use equal amounts in any combination of the following fruits:

Red apples, unpeeled and diced*	Nectarines, diced	Strawberries, hulled and quartered or sliced
Apricots, peeled and diced	Oranges, sectioned and diced	Seedless grapes
Banana slices*	Grapefruit, sectioned and diced	Superfine sugar, optional
Blueberries	Peaches, peeled and diced	Orange liqueur
Cherries, pitted and halved	Pears, peeled and diced*	Chopped nuts, optional
Red currants	Pineapple, diced	Sweetened whipped cream
Kiwi fruit, peeled and sliced	Raspberries	

Combine prepared fruit in a glass bowl. Sprinkle with a little sugar, if desired, and add 3 or 4 tablespoons liqueur. Chill for 1 to 2 hours, carefully turning fruit occasionally.

To serve, transfer fruit to a glass serving bowl or individual serving dishes. Sprinkle with chopped nuts, if desired.

Pass a bowl of lightly sweetened whipped cream with salad.

*Sprinkle with lemon juice to prevent discoloration.

Melon Balls a l'Orange

2 tablespoons frozen orange juice concentrate, thawed
2 tablespoons orange liqueur
2 cups honeydew melon balls
2 cups cantaloupe balls
1 cup medium strawberries, hulled

Blend together orange juice and liqueur. Place fruit in a glass bowl. Spoon orange juice mixture over fruit. Refrigerate for several hours, stirring occasionally.

Drain fruit before serving in individual glass bowls.

Makes 4 servings

Strawberries Romanoff

1 quart fresh strawberries,
  washed and hulled
2 tablespoons granulated sugar
2 tablespoons orange juice
2 to 3 tablespoons orange
  liqueur
  Sweetened whipped cream

Place strawberries in a shallow bowl. Sprinkle with sugar. Stir together orange juice and liqueur; pour over berries. Cover and refrigerate until chilled. To serve, divide berries and accumulated juice among individual serving dishes. Top with a rosette of whipped cream.

Makes 4 servings

Pineapple Black Forest Style

1 ripe pineapple, peeled,
  quartered, and sliced
  Framboise or kirsch
  Powdered sugar
  Sweetened whipped cream
  Fresh strawberries dipped in
  melted chocolate or chocolate
  curls

In a glass bowl, combine pineapple and framboise to taste. Sprinkle with powdered sugar to taste. Refrigerate for about 2 hours. To serve, drain pineapple slices. Arrange in a wreath on individual serving plates. Sprinkle with a little of the accumulated juices. Pipe a large rosette of sweetened whipped cream in the center. Top with a chocolate-dipped strawberry or chocolate curls.

Makes 4 servings

Surprise Oranges

3 large, firm-skinned oranges
1 tablespoon unflavored gelatin
3 egg yolks
⅔ cup powdered sugar
  Grated peel of ½ lemon
3 tablespoons orange liqueur
1½ cups whipping cream

Cut oranges in half and carefully scoop out pulp; reserve shells. Squeeze juice from pulp to measure ½ cup. Sprinkle gelatin over orange juice; let stand to soften.

In the top of a double boiler, beat egg yolks, powdered sugar, and lemon peel until thick and light-colored. Add orange mixture and beat until gelatin dissolves. Remove from heat. Beat until lukewarm. Blend in liqueur. Refrigerate for 10 to 15 minutes but do not allow to set.

In a bowl, beat cream until stiff. Fold in orange cream. Refrigerate until mixture mounds when dropped from a spoon. Spoon into orange halves and refrigerate until firm. Serve on cracked ice.

Makes 6 servings

Fruit Salad, page 77

Index

Approximate Equivalents for Basic Foods

Food	Metric	American	Food	Metric	American
Almonds (whole)	150 grams	1 cup	Gelatin		
Baking powder	4.3 grams	1 teaspoon (approx.)	(leaf sheets)	6 medium size leaves	2 tablespoons
	30 grams	2½ tablespoons	(granulated)	150 grams	1 cup
Bread crumbs			Meats	500 grams	1 pound (generous)
(dry)	90 grams	1 cup	(diced)	226 grams	1 cup
(fresh)	45 grams	1 cup	Pepper		
Butter	15 grams	1 tablespoon	(whole white)	30 grams	3⅝ tablespoons
	125 grams	½ cup	(whole black)	30 grams	4½ tablespoons
	500 grams	2 cups	(powdered)	30 grams	4 tablespoons
Cheese	500 grams	1 pound (generous)	Raisins		
			(seeded)	12 grams	1 tablespoon
(grated)	100 grams	1 cup (scant)		200 grams	1 cup
Coffee			(seedless)	10 grams	1 tablespoon
(medium ground)	85 grams	1 cup		160 grams	1 cup
				500 grams	3 cups
Cornstarch	10 grams	1 tablespoon	Rice	240 grams	1 cup
Cream of tartar	3-4 grams	1 teaspoon	Salt	15 grams	1 tablespoon
Fish	500 grams	1 pound (generous)	Spices (ground)	2½ grams	1 teaspoon
				15 grams	2 tablespoons
Flour			Sugar		
(unsifted, all purpose)	35 grams	¼ cup	(fine granulated)	5 grams	1 teaspoon
	70 grams	½ cup		15 grams	1 tablespoon
	142 grams	1 cup		60 grams	¼ cup
	500 grams	3½ cups		240 grams	1 cup
(sifted, all purpose)	32 grams	¼ cup	(confectioners' or icing)		
	60 grams	½ cup		35 grams	¼ cup
	128 grams	1 cup		70 grams	½ cup
(sifted, cake and pastry)				140 grams	1 cup
	30 grams	¼ cup	(brown)	10 grams	1 tablespoon
	60 grams	½ cup		80 grams	½ cup
	120 grams	1 cup		160 grams	1 cup
Fruit			Vegetables		
(fresh)	500 grams	1 pound (generous)	(fresh)	500 grams	1 pound (generous)
(dried)	500 grams	2 cups	(dried)	500 grams	2 cups

EUROPEAN DESSERTS

Rich and elegant desserts, specialties of European chefs, can now be made easily in your own kitchen with the help of our *European Desserts* cookbook. Here are the secrets of the European pastry-chef's trade: hints to guide you to spectacular results, decorating ideas for finishing touches, special flavorings, and basic recipes with a wealth of variations.

For an afternoon tea or an after-theater gathering, or for any occasion that needs a grand finale, choose one or several of these impressive delicacies. Our selections include:

- Cakes, Tortes, and Flans: Swiss Kirsch Torte, Kiwi Fruit Flan, Refrigerator Cheesecake...

- Pastries and Small Sweets: Hazelnut Petit Fours, Almond Horns, Pineapple Napoleons...

- Frozen Desserts: Macadamia Ice Cream, Raspberry Sorbet, Coffee Strawberry Bombe...

Plus — tarts, cookies, confections, and more! Delectable, delicious, and waiting for you — *European Desserts*.

ideals

0-8249-3029-0

US $4.95
Canada $6.50